The Asylum Workshop

Colin Murphy

T0026962

methuen | drama

LONDON • NEW YORK • OXFORD • NEW DELHI • SYDNEY

METHUEN DRAMA
Bloomsbury Publishing Plc
50 Bedford Square, London, WC1B 3DP, UK
1385 Broadway, New York, NY 10018, USA
29 Earlsfort Terrace, Dublin 2, Ireland

BLOOMSBURY, METHUEN DRAMA and the Methuen
Drama logo are trademarks of Bloomsbury Publishing Plc

First published in Great Britain 2023

A catalogue record for this book is available from the British Library.

A catalog record for this book is available from the Library of Congress.

ISBN: PB: 978-1-3504-2973-4
ePDF: 978-1-3504-2975-8
eBook: 978-1-3504-2974-1

Series: Modern Plays

Typeset by Mark Heslington Ltd, Scarborough, North Yorkshire

To find out more about our authors and books visit
www.bloomsbury.com and sign up for our newsletters.

Technological University Dublin Conservatoire
and Grangegorman Histories present

The Asylum Workshop

*Fragments from the archive of the institution once
known as Grangegorman Lunatic Asylum*

By Colin Murphy with the final-year Technological University
Dublin B.A. (Hons) in Drama (Performance) students

The Asylum Workshop: Fragments from the archive of the institution once known as Grangegorman Lunatic Asylum by Colin Murphy with the final-year B.A. (Hons) in Drama (Performance) students was first produced by Technological University Dublin and Grangegorman Histories in the East Quad Black Box Theatre on 15 December 2022 with the following cast and production team:

Cast (in alphabetical order)

Ibironke Akigbogun
Darragh Barron
Chloe Bassett
Luke Collins
Lauren Dignam
Bronagh Donaghey
Conor Farrell
Shane Griffin
Eva Hunter
Donagh Lynch
Páraic Mac Lochlainn
Paul Mahady
Kevin Maher
Emily Mc Alinden
Luke Mc Mahon
Oscar Meagher
Sarah Taylor Mooney
Seán Norton
Evie May O'Brien
James Ronan
Simone Sowell
Quinton Walker
Fergus Whyte

Production Team

Director & Producer: Peter McDermott
Playwright: Colin Murphy
Costume & Set Designer: Sinéad O'Donnell-Carey
Lighting Designer: Matt Burke
Sound Designer: Aoife Kavanagh
Dramaturg: Tanya Dean
Stage Manager: Tamar Keane
Intimacy Coordinator: Sue Mythen

Dialect Coach: Cathal Quinn
Assistant Stage Manager: Ruby Collin
Costume Supervisor: Niamh O'Brien
Lighting Operator: Aoibheann Moriarty
Set Builder: Robert Ryan
Technical Manager: Cormac Carroll
Events Manager: Lisa O'Brien
Production Photographer: Conor Mulhern
Academic Consultant: Professor Brendan Kelly, Professor of
Psychiatry at Trinity College Dublin

The Asylum Workshop runs for approximately one hour and forty
minutes (not including intermission).

Content Warning: This play refers to and represents mental health
issues and different forms of treatment (including electroconvulsive
therapy and involuntary admission), and many historical treatments
that may seem barbaric to contemporary audiences. The play features
a scene depicting convulsions, and scenes including references to
abortifacients, domestic abuse, sexual abuse, and Magdalene
Laundries. In addition, original language, and terminology from the
past and from various archives and reports are maintained. This
reflects an attempt to remain faithful to historical sources and does not
signify any endorsement of the broader use of such terminology in
contemporary settings.

Cast

Ibironke Akigbogun

Darragh Barron

Chloe Bassett

Luke Collins

Lauren Dignam

Bronagh Donaghey

Conor Farrell

Shane Griffin

Eva Hunter

Donagh Lynch

Páraic Mac Lochlainn

Paul Mahady

Cast

Kevin Maher

Emily Mc Alinden

Luke Mc Mahon

Oscar Meagher

Sarah Mooney

Seán Norton

Evie May O'Brien

James Ronan

Simone Sowell

Quinton Walker

Fergus Whyte

Cast photos courtesy of Bachelor of Arts (Honours) in Photography Year 2 students, Technological University Dublin

Playwright's Note

This play is based on the history of the psychiatric institution at Grangegorman, as told in the hospital's archives, in secondary sources and in personal interviews with former patients, staff and academics. The hospital's archive has been deposited in the National Archives, where it is available to consult (subject to rules regarding privacy and non-disclosure). This archive is an extraordinary part of our national heritage and this process of protecting it and opening it to the public was what made this play possible. My access was facilitated by Professor Brendan Kelly, who was a sounding board throughout the process, and Brian Donnelly.

Where dates are signalled in the play, they are accurate. Where the dates are vague (e.g. 'early 1800s'), that is because I have combined distinct events into one scene. Where patient names are used, they are pseudonyms. Where locations are mentioned, they have sometimes been changed, for privacy. Where archive material has been used, it is largely verbatim, but has been edited and sometimes rephrased for clarity and economy. This is a history play, which is to say it is a play first, and history second. Playwriting (like all narrative writing), when based on fact, requires simplification, elision, conflation and occasionally outright anachronism. Examine the historical timeline of the 1810s closely and you will find the version here to be a travesty: Francis Johnston's GPO was built after the asylum, for example. What we hope to achieve, in ninety minutes on stage, is something that feels truthful even as that truth inevitably evades us. (More on this in the Afterword.)

The shape of the play was inspired by the students here performing it (alongside some absent classmates), who workshopped early material; it was deftly shepherded to its final shape by director Peter McDermott and dramaturg Tanya Dean, whose moral support, as well as dramatic insight, were crucial. Both the commissioning of the play, in the first instance, and this revival as a professional production, in the second, were considerable acts of faith by TU Dublin and Grangegorman Histories in the importance of this story and in our capacity to translate it to stage. I am grateful to them.

Colin Murphy, playwright

Director's Note

There is an old Japanese ritual in which the new inhabitants of a building or site stomp rhythmically on the floor or ground of that site to acknowledge the spirits of those who traversed it before them. It is both an act of commemoration and a way of moving forward: we must address the past before we can formulate our future. I came across this tradition when researching theatre director Tadashi Suzuki, who draws on the stomping ritual in his actor training, to develop an actor's physical rootedness and presence. This was the impetus for this production.

Grangegorman Histories is a public history project with the remit of cataloguing and memorializing the history of this site. When dramaturg Tanya Dean and I approached them with the idea of creating a play about the Grangegorman psychiatric hospital for TU Dublin's final-year Drama students, they very generously offered us funding, which enabled us to commission playwright Colin Murphy.

Colin's track record in documentary drama is second to none in Ireland. His forensic searches in the Grangegorman Archives and published histories quickly revealed the paucity of patients' voices, raising the question of whose story we were telling. He also engaged the TU Dublin students in workshops and improvisations to ensure that their voices – the future of Ireland addressing Ireland's past – were part of the story.

In addition to support from Prof Brendan Kelly and Brian Donnelly, we are indebted to artist Dr Christina Henri and also artist Alan Counihan, whose RTÉ radio documentary *The Ghosts of Grangegorman* was crucial in our research. Thank you also to the ex-patients, ex-staff and others connected to the hospital who kindly offered their stories and experiences.

With this performance, we offer you our version of a stomping ritual. May we move into the future more wisely by acknowledging the rich and troubled past of this site.

Peter McDermott, director

Note from Technological University Dublin

When walking through the leafy campus of Technological University Dublin in Grangegorman, there is a sense of the past meeting the present; the modern architecture of a twenty-first-century university sits companionably alongside stately stone buildings that date from the early 1800s. For the thousands of TU Dublin staff and students who cross this campus every day, elegant edifices like Rathdown House, the Clock Tower and Lower House serve as daily reminders that Grangegorman occupies a storied space in the history of Ireland. Over the course of 250 years (before it became the home of TU Dublin), this site was host to a penitentiary, a workhouse, and a variety of incarnations of mental healthcare institutions – the Richmond Lunatic Asylum, a shell-shock hospital post-World War I, the Grangegorman Mental Hospital, and St Brendan's Hospital.

In this production and in this script, we see a detailed and emotionally-affecting portrait of that history of Grangegorman, giving voice to the past incarnations of these buildings – and, most importantly, to those who dwelled within them – with dignity and compassion. Along with Grangegorman Histories, TU Dublin Conservatoire was proud to support this artistic endeavour to explore the archives of the site upon which our institution now stands. Colin Murphy's conscientious research and empathetic storytelling offers a nuanced perspective on this complicated history, bought vividly to life by the talented students of the 2023 class of the B.A. (Hons) in Drama (Performance), and directed with skill and sensitivity by Peter McDermott. Today, as TU Dublin prepares students for a future of infinite possibilities, *The Asylum Workshop* allows us an opportunity to also acknowledge and honour the past.

The Conservatoire is deeply grateful to Professor David FitzPatrick (President, TU Dublin), Dr Orla McDonagh (Dean, Faculty of Arts and Humanities), the Grangegorman Development Agency and Grangegorman Histories, whose support was instrumental in the development of *The Asylum Workshop*.

Note from Grangegorman Histories

The buildings of Grangegorman stand as physical monuments to the past and the complex histories of the site. Less tangible are the records of the people and practices associated with these buildings. Through our diverse programme of events, publications and learning opportunities, Grangegorman Histories aims to uncover such records and give a voice to the voiceless. We were delighted, therefore, to support TU Dublin Conservatoire by providing the funding necessary to commission a professional playwright. And even more delighted when Colin Murphy, a playwright of such stature, agreed to take on the role.

Having seen this play performed, we commend all involved for producing a work of great power and authenticity. It tells important stories of Grangegorman that need to be heard and which we hope will encourage further discourse about the people who lived there.

Our project has ambitious plans for the future, whereby further activities like this will help us fulfil our mission and achieve our goals. We look forward to engaging with as many people as possible to ensure that we do so.

Please view our website at www.grangegormanhistories.ie if you wish to learn more about the project and to join us on our journey of discovery.

Dr Philip Cohen, Chair of the Expert Working Group

A Select Bibliography for *The Asylum Workshop*

- Damien Brennan, *Irish Insanity 1800–2000*
- Damien Brennan, author interview
- Ivor Browne, *The Psychiatrist: Music and Madness*
- Ivor Browne, *The Writings of Ivor Browne*
- Alan Counihan, author interview
- Alan Counihan, Personal Effects: A History of Possession (exhibition)
- Mary Daly, author interview
- Michel Foucault, *History of Madness*
- Raymond Gillespie, Explore Grangegorman Before the Institutions. https://www.ria.ie/ news/grangegorman-histories/explore-grangegorman-institutions
- Alan Gilsenan, *Meetings with Ivor* (film)
- Grangegorman Histories, interview with Ivor Browne by Alan Gilsenan (video)
- Color Hanratty, The Hamlet Podcast, www.thehamletpodcast.com
- Peter Heaslip, author interview
- Ernest Jones, *Hamlet and Oedipus*
- Brendan Kelly, author interview
- Brendan Kelly, *In Search of Madness*
- Brendan Kelly, *Custody, Care and Criminality: Forensic Psychiatry and Law in 19th Century Ireland*
- James Mary O'Connor, author interview
- James Mary O'Connor, The Transformative Power Of Education, TEDx talk (video)
- James Mary O'Connor (ed.), *Grangegorman: An Urban Quarter with an Open Future: The Grangegorman Masterplan for the HSE, DIT and the Local Community*
- Grace O'Keefe, *Grangegorman Histories: Resources for Further Study*
- Patrick Quinlan, *Walls of Containment: The Architecture and Landscapes of Lunacy*
- Sean O'Casey, *Drums under the Windows*
- PM Prior (ed.), *Asylums, Mental health care and the Irish: Historical studies 1800–2010*
- Markus Reuber, *The Architecture Of Psychological Management: The Irish Asylums (1801–1922)*
- Joseph Reynolds, *Grangegorman: Psychiatric Care in Dublin Since 1815*
- TU Dublin Conservatoire, Stages of Memory project: online talks by Brian Donnelly, Brendan Kelly, Christina Henri (video)
- Interviews with former patients (anonymous)

About Grangegorman Histories

Grangegorman Histories is a public history project of Dublin City Council, Grangegorman Development Agency, Health Service Executive, Local Communities, National Archives, Royal Irish Academy and TU Dublin. The project provides opportunities to contribute to the important work of uncovering, cataloguing, and commemorating the history of Grangegorman and the surrounding area.

For more details on the Grangegorman Histories Project, see www.grangegormanhistories.ie

About Technological University Dublin Conservatoire

TU Dublin Conservatoire – formerly Dublin Institute of Technology Conservatory of Music and Drama – was founded in 1890 as the Dublin Municipal School of Music, with around fifty students. It has grown from being a municipal institution to one that is truly national and international. Now, the Conservatoire provides the highest quality education across the broadest range of performing arts disciplines in Ireland, to more than 1,200 students. The Conservatoire offers a range of highly specialised junior and undergraduate programmes in Classical and Irish Traditional Music, Drama, Keyboard Studies, Jazz, Orchestral Studies, and Vocal and Opera Studies. There is a flourishing postgraduate community, with taught masters in music performance, conducting, musicological and composition research, and opportunities for MPhil and doctorate research in Music or Drama.

For more details on the Conservatoire, see https://www.tudublin.ie/explore/faculties-and-schools/arts-humanities/conservatoire/

About the B.A. (Hons) in Drama (Performance)

The B.A. (Hons) in Drama (Performance) is a three-year, full-time course in practical drama training and education. While practical performance is at the core of the course, students also undertake substantial academic research and analysis, as well as extensive training in drama facilitation. As part of the many modules across three years, students perform in one small-scale production and two large-scale graduating productions (including *The Asylum Workshop* in 2022). The Technological University Dublin Conservatoire has over twenty-five years' experience in drama training and is one of the leading centres of education in the performing arts in Ireland. Graduates have had national and international success as actors, directors, playwrights, drama facilitators and drama researchers.

For more details on the B.A. (Hons) in Drama (Performance), see:

www.tudublin.ie/study/undergraduate/courses/drama-performance-tu962/

The cast, crew and author of *The Asylum Workshop* wish to thank

The family and friends of the cast, the first- and second-year drama students, Lisa O'Brien, Sarah FitzGibbon, Charlotte Tiernan, Russell Smith, Rob Jones, Rachel Talbot, Paul McNulty, Fiona Howard, Kevin Hanafin, Kerry Houston, David Mooney, Fabiola Hand, Anne Marie Fidgeon, Gaia Sessa, Michelle Moloney, Stephen Wallace, Ruth Hegarty, Brendan Kelly, Grangegorman Histories, Grangegorman Development Agency, Alan Counihan, Brian Donnelly, Christina Henri, Aisling Roche, Zoe Reid, Nora Rahill, HSE 'Transport' section Grangegorman, Catriona Crowe, Pól Ó Murchú, James Mary O'Connor, Dark Daughter Costume Hire, Abbey Costume Hire, Des Kelly Interiors, Cathy Addis, Valeria Cavalli, Lisa Saputo, St Vincent's Hospital Estate Services Department, Damien Brennan, Mary Daly, Alan Gilsenan, Peter Heaslip, Michael Larkin, Markus Reuber, and those former patients who spoke to the author in confidence.

The Asylum Workshop

Notes

The play is written for a large cast, with an imperative to distribute lines as widely as possible. Casting in the student scenes is fluid: **Student One** *in one scene need not be the same actor as* **Student One** *in another scene. Lines from* **Student One** *may be given to* **Student Two***, and vice versa. There is room for improvisation in the student scenes, and actors should use their real names when doing so. Similarly, casting of nurses, orderlies, doctors, etc, is fluid – a nurse is one scene (or even later in the same scene) is not necessarily the same character as a nurse in a previous scene.*

Scene titles may be projected above the stage, perhaps accompanied by a sound effect (e.g. a typewriter) for punctuation. Projections may be used both where indictated and to show documents that characters in the play are discussing.

In the original production, there were two defined areas on stage: a small raised platform, upstage left, where the historical scenes took place, and an area with a table, upstage right, where the students did their research. Other scenes made fluid use of the space. An iron hospital bed was brought on as appropriate. The whole play took place against a backdrop of voluminous archives on dusty shelves.

Prologue

As the audience enters, the space is already populated with students preparing for class – running lines, going over scripts, rehearsing, chatting. The house lights are on.

One group of three rehearses a scene from Hamlet. *The actor and director go repeatedly over the soliloquy, while the actress waits to enter the scene, her impatience growing. Classmates watch, and may interject occasionally.*

This all takes place as the audience take their seats. As the audience settles and the house lights dim, the scene finally reaches the moment of the actress's entrance.

Student Actor
> To be, or not to be, that is the question:
> Whether 'tis nobler in the mind to suffer
> The slings and arrows of outrageous fortune,
> Or to take arms against a sea of troubles
> And by opposing end them. To die – to sleep,
> No more; and by a sleep to say we end
> The heart-ache and the thousand natural shocks
> That flesh is heir to: 'tis a consummation
> Devoutly to be wished. To die, to sleep;
> To sleep, perchance to dream – ay, there's the rub;
> For in that sleep of death what dreams may come,
> When we have shuffled off this mortal coil,
> Must give us pause – there's the respect
> That makes calamity of so long life.
> For who would bear the whips and scorns of time,
> The oppressor's wrong, the proud man's contumely,
> The pangs of despised love, the law's delay,
> The insolence of office, and the spurns
> That patient merit of the unworthy takes,
> When he himself might his quietus make
> With a bare bodkin? Who would fardels bear,
> To grunt and sweat under a weary life,
> But that the dread of something after death,
> The undiscovered country, from whose bourn

No traveller returns, puzzles the will,
And makes us rather bear those ills we have
Than fly to others that we know not of?
Thus conscience does make cowards of us all,
And thus the native hue of resolution
Is sicklied o'er with the pale cast of thought,
And enterprises of great pith and moment
With this regard their currents turn awry
And lose the name of action –

Student Actress (*to herself*)   Finally!

Student Actor
Soft you now,
The fair Ophelia!

Student Director (*cutting in*)   Let's go back on that just one more time –

Student Actress   For Christ's sake!

Student Director   Sorry?

Student Actress   We've been doing this for an hour and I haven't even said a line.

Student Director   I'm sorry, we got a bit distracted – by the most famous speech in all of drama.

Student Actress (*under her breath*)   So fucking overrated.

Student Director   What?

Student Actress   Can we *please* run the rest of the scene *once* before class starts.

The **Director** *decides it's not worth the fight. In the meantime, the other students have gathered to watch.*

Student Director   OK. Give her the cue.

Student Actor
Soft you now,
The fair Ophelia! Nymph, in thy orisons
Be all my sins –

What are 'orisons' again?

Student Actress   Christ!

Student Director   Prayers, they're / prayers

Student Actress   Can we just *run* the *scene*?

Student Actor   I need to know what I'm saying!

Student Actress   I haven't got to say *anything*!

Student Director   Cue her.

Student Actor (*desultory*)
Be all my sins remembered.

Student Actress
Good my lord,
How does your honour for this many a day?

She plays it with an unusual abrasiveness – as her actress-self, a woman of 2023, not as a 'Shakespearean' character.

Student Actor
I humbly thank you, well.

Student Actress
My lord, I have remembrances of yours
That I have longed long to re-deliver.
I pray you now receive them.

Student Actor
No, not I.
I never gave you aught.

Student Actress
My honoured lord, you know right well you did
And with them words of so sweet breath composed
As made the things more rich. Their perfume lost,
Take these again; for to the noble mind
Rich gifts wax poor when givers prove unkind.
There, my lord.

Student Actor
Ha, ha! Are you honest?

Student Actress
My lord?

Student Actor
Are you fair?

Student Actress
What means your lordship?

Student Actor
That if you be honest and fair, your honesty should admit no discourse to your beauty.
I did love you once.

Student Actress
Indeed, my lord, you made me believe so.

Student Actor
You should not have believed me: I loved you not.

Student Actress
I was the more deceived.

Student Actor
Get thee to a nunnery. Why wouldst thou be a breeder of sinners? I am myself indifferent honest but yet I could accuse me of such things that it were better my mother had not borne me. I am very proud, revengeful, ambitious, with more offences at my beck than I have thoughts to put them in, imagination to give them shape, or time to act them in –

Student Director (*cutting in*)   OK, that's a big one there, let's go back over that. What's at stake here for Hamlet?

Student Actress   For *Hamlet*? What about Ophelia?

Student Director   Let's not make this all about you –

The other **Students** *roll their eyes at the* **Actress**.

Student One   The play *is* called Hamlet.

Student Actress   It's not about *me*! It's about the stakes. Who has the power here? Hamlet. And who has everything to lose? Ophelia.

Student Director   I think Hamlet's the victim here – his father has just been murdered.

Student Actress   And what's he doing with that 'victimhood'? Transferring it to Ophelia.

Student Two   She's got a point.

Student Three   He's having a breakdown.

Student Actress   He's only fucking pretending!

Student Two   Yeh – who *actually* has a break down in the play? Ophelia.

Student Actress   And what provokes that? Hamlet's gaslighting.

Student Actor (*scornful*)   Gaslighting! Don't be / ridiculous –

Student Actress   'I did love you *once*' . . . 'I loved you *not*.'

Student Two   She gives him back his letters – and he says he never gave her any.

Student Actress   It's the definition of gaslighting.

Some of the male **Students** *object – 'woke nonsense' etc.*

Student Actress (*to the objectors*)   Out there, it's all 'consent workshops' and 'safe spaces'. And then we get in here, and you lot have a hard-on for a bloke who's just another privileged fuckboy who dumps his girlfriend as soon as he gets her up the pole!

Noisy disagreement from the crowd.

Student Four   Up the pole?

Student Actress (*like it's obvious*)   The flowers she gives out?

Student Actor   They're just fucking flowers.

Student Actress   She gives them *rue*.

Student Five   She's batshit – isn't that the point?

Student Actress   Rue was an abortion drug.

More disagreement from the crowd.

Student Two   Really?

Student Six (*impressed*)   No way.

Student Actor   Oh come   **Student Director**   That's a bit
on –   tenuous –

Student Actress (*over them*)   'A *breeder* of sinners'? 'Get thee
to a *nunnery*'?

Student Director   He doesn't mean it literally –

Student Actress   Doesn't mean it? He's the fucking prince.
He's one of the wealthiest, most powerful men in the
country. He tells a girl he's got pregnant he's going to send
her to a – a Magdalene Laundry – and she's supposed to
think it's a joke?

This quiets them.

What would happen if we played this scene like Hamlet was
Harvey Weinstein, not Ed fucking Sheeran?

Student Director   *OK*, let's give it a try. We'll go / from
Ophelia's entrance.

The **Teacher** *bursts in to the theatre, carrying a box.*

Teacher   Good morning everybody, sorry I'm late, sorry
I'm late.

The Beginning

Teacher   I have an announcement to make . . .

Excited murmuring amongst the **Students***.*

Teacher   Yes, it's the end of term show.

'Drum roll.'

The TU Dublin Conservatoire class of 2023 will be
presenting as their final performance . . .

The **Students** *call out their favourite dramatists' names hopefully.*

Teacher   a documentary drama . . .

Groans all round.

Teacher   based on your own research . . .

The groans overflow into protest.

Teacher   into the history of the institution around you.

Puzzled silence.

Student Two   The history of TU Dublin?

Teacher   The history of Grangegorman.

Student Three   What, like, the old church and stuff?

Teacher   The hospital.

Student Four   What hospital?

Teacher   The old asylum.

Student Five   This was an asylum?

Student Six   I *knew* this place was a madhouse.

Laughter.

Teacher   The walls around you –

He looks at the walls, and corrects himself.

Well, OK, not these walls – but the *old* walls on campus – the
Clock Tower building – the Lower House, down there where
the Students' Union is – they were built to house the
country's first national, public lunatic asylum –

Student Four   That's a bit objectifying.

Teacher   That was the language of the time – it's still
engraved on the building.

Student Four   I'm not very comfortable with it.

Teacher   Well you're going to have plenty of time to explore that, because you're going to make a play about it.

He opens the box and starts distributing books.

Start with these. For next session, I want everyone to prepare notes for a scene to be devised in class, based on a factual moment in the history of this hospital.

The **Students** *set to discussing the project, and reading, in small groups. Meanwhile, another area on stage becomes:*

Dublin Castle – Early 1800s

The **Lord Lieutenant** *is at his desk.*

Chief Secretary (*entering*)   Lord Lieutenant.

Lord Lieutenant   Ah, Chief Secretary, good to have you back. What's the word from London? What's occupying them in the House of Commons?

Chief Secretary   I'm rather afraid Ireland is, Sir.

Lord Lieutenant   Ah.

Chief Secretary   I attended at the hearings of the Select Committee on the Lunatic Poor in Ireland. The member for Mayo – he spoke about how the peasants of his county react when they have a case of madness in the family.

Denis Browne MP (*addressing the parliamentary committee*) The only way they have to manage is by making a hole in the floor of their cabin not high enough for the person to stand up in, with a crib over it to prevent his getting up. The hole is about five feet deep, and they give the wretched being his food there, and there he generally dies.

Lord Lieutenant   Good God, the barbarities of the Irish peasant never cease to astonish me. Why don't these people build prisons for their lunatics, like any civilised society?

Chief Secretary   Well . . . we build the prisons, Lord Lieutenant.

Lord Lieutenant   Ah. Yes. Of course.

Chief Secretary   And I am afraid they are all overcrowded. In fact, one of the governors of the Limerick workhouse addressed the Select Committee on that very point.

Workhouse Governor (*addressing the committee*)   When the keepers have to restrain someone who is disturbed, there is no room to separate them from the rest, so they pass their hands under the inmate's knees, fasten them with manacles, fasten both about their ankles, pass a chain over all, and then fasten them to a bed. The overcrowding is so bad, sometimes they find corpses that have been days without being removed.

Lord Lieutenant   Are you suggesting we *do* something, Chief Secretary?

Chief Secretary   Well, that is what the Select Committee is recommending.

Lord Lieutenant   Yes?

Chief Secretary   They believe the country should have a dedicated institution to house the lunatic poor.

Lord Lieutenant   What, like a workhouse for the mad?

Chief Secretary   Something like that, Lord Lieutenant.

Lord Lieutenant   What an intriguing idea. Where would we put it?

Meeting With a Historian

The **Teacher** *leads in the* **Historian**.

Teacher   I thought it would be helpful to your research to have a series of talks from experts in this area. We're going to start with a Historian.

Student One   Hasn't the 'Historian' got a name?

Teacher   Well, this is a theatrical representation of the research process, right? So this is a generic historian – a composite – based on reading and talking to a few different historians.

Historian   'Generic historian'?

Teacher   Right.

Historian   Is that a character note?

Teacher   Can we just get on with it?

Historian   Right. So this story starts with the Vikings.

Student Two   This is looking up.

Historian (*with relish*)   Sitric Silkbeard.

She starts a slide show with illustrations and maps.

Historian   Viking ruler of Dublin, a thousand years ago. In the year 1030, Christ Church is founded, across the river, and he grants the lands around us here in Grangegorman to the church.

So over the centuries, as suburban Dublin expands, and particularly in the seventeenth and eighteenth centuries when Smithfield and Stoneybatter are developed, Grangegorman remains rural. Farmland and woodland. It's also a bit higher than the city, and it's known for its good air. So as the city grows up around it, it becomes a kind of rural retreat – an escape from the city.

This is it in 1811 . . . There's the river, and Smithfield just above it – King Street – Brunswick Street – and then Grangegorman – you can see how it suddenly leaves the city behind – it's just a country lane with mostly fields on either side . . .

So not only does Grangegorman have land and space, but it also has an association in the public mind with good health.

And then the Administration – Dublin Castle – comes looking for a site to build the country's first national, public asylum . . .

Dublin Castle

The **Chief Secretary** *leads* **Francis Johnston** *in to the office.*

Chief Secretary   Lord Lieutenant, I've brought the architect, Mr Francis Johnston, to discuss the design of the new lunatic asylum.

Lord Lieutenant   Ah! Very good. Mr Johnston!

Francis Johnston (*shaking hands*)   Lord Lieutenant.

Lord Lieutenant   I say, congratulations on your new General Post Office.

Chief Secretary   Oh yes, it's a marvellous construction.

Francis Johnston   Thank you, gentlemen.

Lord Lieutenant   Like the pyramids – built to last a thousand years, eh?

Francis Johnston   One can only hope.

Chief Secretary   A beacon for the Empire.

Lord Lieutenant   Speaking of imperial benevolence – the asylum. Have you thought of a name for it yet?

Francis Johnston   Why, Lord Lieutenant, I thought we could name it after you.

Chief Secretary   The 'Lord Lieutenant'?

Lord Lieutenant (*correcting him*)   The Duke of Richmond.

Francis Johnston   The Richmond Lunatic Asylum. Has a nice ring, don't you think?

Lord Lieutenant   Oh I do. Now, how go the plans?

Francis Johnston   There are some very interesting ideas being developed across the water . . .

Lord Lieutenant   Yes?

Francis Johnston   The York Retreat has come up with the idea of letting the lunatics out of their cells.

Lord Lieutenant   How extraordinary. But how ever do you ensure order?

Francis Johnston   A chap named Bentham has a solution to that – Jeremy Bentham.

As he shows the **Lord Lieutenant** *plans, they appear as projections.*

Lord Lieutenant   Yes?

Francis Johnston   He calls it the Panopticon.

Lord Lieutenant   'Panopticon.'

Francis Johnston   Greek mythology. Panoptes. Giant with a hundred eyes – 'all-seeing'.

Lord Lieutenant   Indeed.

Francis Johnston   The prison – or asylum – is built in wings around a central core. This central core is occupied by the staff – the guards, orderlies, nurses. At a glance, they can see into every wing, down every corridor. The prisoner – or the inmate – knows they are being watched and modulates their behaviour accordingly. This promotes reform – or recovery. That is one possible design . . .

Chief Secretary   And the other?

Francis Johnston   A traditional institution. Four wings enclosing a courtyard.

Lord Lieutenant (*approvingly*)   A courtyard. Good for exercise, no?

Francis Johnston   Quite.

Lord Lieutenant   Though, it would be convenient to be able to separate inmates – men and women, lunatics and idiots, that kind of thing . . .

Chief Secretary   I wonder is there some kind of compromise to be made . . .

Francis Johnston   Compromise?

Chief Secretary   Well, if you took the traditional structure, with its courtyard, and added a central axis to it – rather like your panopticon . . .

They pour over the plans together.

Meeting With a Historian (Cont'd)

The **Historian** *resumes the slideshow.*

Historian   So this is the plan for the original Richmond Lunatic Asylum, which we now call the Lower House. When you go out onto the concourse, it's the building you can see down to the left. All that remains is the front section – the rest was beyond saving and had to be demolished. When you sit down in the canteen that's there, now, you can see where the original cell walls were – between the windows.

Then, in 1820, they add a prison – that's the Clock Tower building. Over the years, it's used as a cholera hospital, and then for holding women and children who have been sentenced to transportation to Van Diemen's Land . . .

(*Aside.*) There'd be a play in that.

And then it too becomes part of the asylum. Because the asylum is *always* overcrowded.

And so they expand across the road, adding a new asylum building, two churches – one Catholic, one Protestant – and a mortuary. And so Grangegorman becomes this vast institutional complex. It gets renamed in the 1950s, as St Brendan's Hospital, but everybody just calls it 'the Gorman'.

And then, in the late twentieth century, this kind of institutionalised psychiatric care falls out of fashion, and the Gorman is slowly wound down. It finally closes in 2013.

Encountering the Archive

The **Teacher** *enters. He brings with him a trolley stacked high with archive boxes and crates. They are battered and dusty. Perhaps there are more than he can manage and he asks for help carting them in.*

Teacher   When the hospital closed down, it left behind a huge archive. It seems nobody knew what to do with it. Not just files, but stuff – stuff that was in the hospital's stores.

He starts to distribute the boxes; the students come over to take them.

Teacher   They're working out what to do with it and, in the meantime, I've borrowed some of it. I thought it could make for some useful prompts, for improv exercises.

The **Students** *collect the boxes and begin to explore their contents.*

Claire Keeley's Story: Inns Quay Police Court – 1908

The **Divisional Justice** *sits behind a desk.* **Claire Keeley** *stands before him, hands bound and chafing, accompanied by the* **Medical Officer** *and her husband,* **Thomas.** *The* **Justice** *takes a form.*

Justice (*to the* **Medical Officer**)   Lunatic or Idiot?

Medical Officer   Lunatic.

Justice (*indicating* **Thomas**)   And this is?

Medical Officer   The husband.

Justice (*to* **Thomas**)   Your wife's name?

Thomas   Claire. Claire Keeley.

Justice   And you are?

Thomas   Thomas. Your Honour. Thomas Keeley.

Justice   There's no need for the formalities, Mr Keeley –
this is just a police court.

Thomas   Thank you, Your – (*Correcting himself.*) Eh –

Justice   'Sir' will be fine.

Thomas   Sir.

Justice   Address?

Thomas   33 Bridge Street.

Justice   Age?

Thomas (*confused*)   My *age*?

Justice   Your wife's age.

Thomas   Of course. Twenty-eight.

Justice   Religion?

Thomas   Catholic – Roman Catholic.

Justice   Children?

Thomas   Two.

Justice   Education?

Thomas   Yes. She can read and write.

Justice (*finishing that page*)   Very good.

(*To the* **Medical Officer**. *Next page.*) Now. Species of insanity?

Medical Officer   Delusional.

Justice   Any near relative been insane?

The **Medical Officer** *looks to* **Thomas**.

Thomas   A cousin was in the Richmond – for a short time.
She got well – then she went foreign.

Justice (*noting it all*)   Very good.

(*To the* **Medical Officer**.) Cause of derangement?

Medical Officer   Prolonged lactation, I suspect.

Justice   Ah. What age are the children?

Thomas   Three and a year and eight months.

Justice   Now, Mr Keeley – describe what happened.

Thomas   She was always hard working, Your, eh – at the sewing machine late and early. I never noticed anything wrong with her –

Justice   Till?

Thomas   There was a bit of a fight with a neighbour. And the neighbour, she accuses my wife of having had children before she was married – three children – which I myself knows to be false. It's soon after that I start to notice her . . . rambling . . . Saying things that don't make sense . . . Something about a revolver . . .

Justice (*underlining it*)   A revolver.

Thomas   and a Lord Bellew – Bellew is her maiden name. But there's no lords in the family –

Justice (*to himself*)   No.

Thomas   and there being people from Australia in the house.

Justice   And I take it there were not any people from Australia in the house.

Thomas   No.

The **Justice** *makes a final note on the form and passes it to the* **Medical Officer**, *who signs it and passes it back.*

Justice   Very well.

He takes a new form.

He clears his throat.

(*Reading from the form, with formality.*) It has been proved to my satisfaction that

(*Checks the name again.*) Claire Keeley, who is now charged before me, has been discovered and apprehended at

(*Checking it.*) 33 Bridge Street, under circumstances denoting a derangement of mind, and a purpose of committing an indictable crime, that is to say on the seventeenth day of December of 1908 the person charged as aforesaid did, eh . . . (*Thinking it through.*) threaten to shoot

Thomas *wishes to interject but the* **Medical Officer** *silently counsels him not to.*

Justice   . . . some person or persons unknown.

And whereas I have seen and examined the said person so charged, and am satisfied that the person so charged is now a dangerous lunatic, I therefore direct, in the name of His Majesty King Edward VII, that the said Lunatic shall forthwith be taken to the Richmond District Lunatic Asylum, there safely to be kept until discharged by due course of law.

Given under my hand and Seal, at Inns Quay Police Court, 19th day of December 1908.

He signs his name to it.

(*Dismissing them.*) Very good.

He hands the form to the **Medical Officer**, *who leads* **Claire** *away, followed by* **Thomas**, *and makes to leave himself.*

Justice (*afterthought*)   Oh, Mr Keeley?

Thomas   Yes, Your Honour – Sir.

Justice   Good luck.

They leave.

'Our Cherub'

The **Students** *remove items from the boxes.*

Student One   Handbags.

Student Two   An umbrella.

Student Three   Letters . . .

Student Four   Some kind of necklace . . .

Student Five   They're rosary beads.

Student Four   A what?

Student Five   For praying!

Student Two   A comb.

Student One   What are these all doing here?

Student Three (*inspecting the letters*)   I think I may have the answer.

The letter writers appear elsewhere on stage. Meanwhile, the **Students** *continue pulling items out of the boxes, corresponding to those cited in the letters.*

Student Three (*reading a letter*)
    Dear Sir . . .

Patient One
    Could you kindly let me have my comb taken from clothing on entry?

Mother
    Dear Sir,
    My son John has asked me to send him a safety razor. Is this permissible?

Student Four (*lifting out dentures*)   Ughhh – teeth?!

Patient Two
    Sir,
    I will be obliged if you will authorise the selection of my small belongings including dentures and belt, nail file, pen, etc.

Aunt
    Dear Sir,
    My nephew went in there on Friday last. Does he need a change of underwear? If he does, I will send some.

Daughter
I wonder could I send my father a little parcel with a few cigarettes, as I know he likes a cigarette.

PS. I am enclosing an envelope so no one will know where the reply comes from.

One of the **Students** *produces a small envelope and takes out a ring.*

Husband
Dear Sir,
The office was closed when my wife was leaving the hospital.

His **Wife** *joins him and takes his hand.*

Husband
Please send her wedding ring to the address below.

Student Two *opens an envelope to find a photo.*

Student Two   A photo. It's a child – a girl. In a summer dress.

Student Four   There's something written on the back.

The **Father** *steps forward, taking a folded photo out of his pocket. He looks at it and runs his thumb over it. Elsewhere:*

Mother
What do you think of our cherub? Isn't she a big fat lump. Full of mischief. She will be five on July 30th.

The **Father** *remains, touching the photo. The* **Students** *find more letters, in bundles.*

Student One   I can't read the handwriting.

Student Five   There's a reply to someone from the hospital here, but without the original it's impossible to know what it's about.

While this has been happening, one of the **Students** *has found a letter of interest, and approached the* **Teacher** *with it.*

Teacher (*private conversation*)   We'll leave that till later. We need some context, first.

Student Two   What are we even looking for?

Student One   A story.

Student Three   But these are just . . . fragments.

Meanwhile, **Student Four** *has taken a large, leather-bound, cobweb-covered ledger from a box.*

Student Four   Look at this.

Student Five   What's that?

Student Four (*reading the cover*)   'Female Case Book – 1908.'

(*Looking through it.*) It seems to be where they recorded admissions.

They turn the pages. The **Students** *continue to comb through the archives throughout the following.*

Claire Keeley's Story: Richmond Lunatic Asylum – 1908

The **Medical Officer** *delivers* **Claire** *to the* **Nurse** *and* **Assistant**, *hands over her committal warrant, and leaves.* **Thomas** *accompanies her, but is separated from her, to be questioned by the* **Administrator**.

The following process should be carried out with military efficiency and precision, but also with care.

Nurse (*checking the warrant*)   Claire Keeley. She'll be . . .

Checking her file.

193 – 08.

The **Nurse** *takes* **Claire**'*s possessions off her and hands them to the* **Assistant**, *who logs them and places them aside.*

Assistant   Wedding ring . . . Miraculous medal (*etc.*)

The **Nurse** *undresses her and commences a medical assessment. She dictates her notes to the* **Assistant** *as she goes.*

Nurse   Eight stone six pounds . . .

No significant injuries . . . or markings . . .

Bruises on each wrist . . .

Assistant   From restraint . . .?

Nurse   Probably.

She continues, checking **Claire***'s eyes and ears.*

Nurse   Open up.

She pries open **Claire***'s mouth.*

Nurse   Eyes, ears, throat all normal . . .

She feels her glands.

Nurse   Enlarged gland under left angle of jaw . . . Stick out your tongue.

Claire *does so.*

Nurse   Tongue moist, flaccid . . .

She puts on a stethoscope and listens to **Claire***'s lungs . . .*

Nurse   Lungs clear . . .

Heart: mitral murmur, systolic and post-systolic.

Assistant   Is that a problem?

Nurse   Not particularly. No cause for alarm.

She puts a hospital gown on **Claire***.*

On the other side of the partition, as this is happening, **Thomas** *is questioned.*

Administrator   Has your wife suffered from any of the following, Mr Keeley? Convulsions in infancy?

Thomas   I know not.

Administrator   Any injuries or shocks?

Thomas   None.

Administrator   Any fevers?

Thomas   Typhoid.

Administrator   Rheumatism?

Thomas   No.

Administrator   Consumption?

Thomas   No.

Administrator   Epilepsy?

Thomas   No.

Administrator   Intemperance?

Thomas   She's always been very temperate.

Administrator   Any other ailments?

Thomas   None.

Administrator   Any peculiarity at all?

Thomas   None.

Administrator   And her mental health?

Thomas   Always good. Till now.

On the other side of the partition, the assessment of **Claire** *is complete. They usher her out.*

Administrator   Thank you, Mr Keeley.

Thomas   Will I be able to see her?

Administrator   You may apply for a visitor pass for Saturday afternoons.

Thomas   And the children – When will I be able to take her home? Will it be weeks?

*Pause. The **Administrator** doesn't answer.*

Thomas (*anxious*)   Months?

Administrator   She will be here as long as she needs, Mr Keeley. We'll take good care of her.

'Locked Up All Day Long'

*The **Students** continue going through the letters.*

Throughout the play, the letters may be announced by projected titles or by the students introducing them, e.g. 'This is from a patient's sister, in York Street', or the letters may simply speak for themselves.

Mother in Donnycarney

Dear Sir,
I am writing this letter on behalf of my son. He escaped about two weeks ago and came home to me. His young brother was ill at the time. Now, up to the time of his escape he was a model patient and gave no trouble whatsoever. He told me he escaped because he was so worried over his brother. I wonder if you would consider giving him his liberty again – I am afraid that his nerves will go bad locked up all day long in the one room.

Mother in Pearse St

I would like to make an application to take my son out of St Brendan's because I don't think that there is any thing mentally wrong with him. There was a bit of family trouble and his wife put him into hospital.

Sister in York St

I am making this application for the discharge of my brother. My husband and myself have been in several times to see him and would like him home. That is his wish.

PS. As we are bad at writing, a friend is doing this for us.

*A **Doctor** and **Secretary** arrive to establish an office, and proceed to deal with correspondence.*

Mother in Fatima Mansions
My son has been transferred down to St Ita's Hospital, Portrane. I would be very grateful if you would have him sent back to St Brendan's Hospital as my health is not too good and I cannot go down to see my son. In St Brendan's we can visit him and take him home on week ends.

Doctor (*dictating*)
I regret that it is not possible at present to have your son transferred back from St Ita's Hospital.

Yours faithfully, etc.

Sister in Thomas St
I would be thankful if it be in your power to transfer my sister back as soon as possible to St Brendan's as my father is an old-age pensioner and cannot make it out to visit her and I am sure she is wondering what's wrong as he visits her every week for the past ten years.

Doctor
I regret that it is not possible at present to have your sister transferred back from St Ita's Hospital.

Mother in Thomas St
I am writing on behalf of my son who was a patient at this hospital. I understood and he going there that he would be kept. But he has been removed without consulting me. I find it very difficult to go out so far to see him as my means does not allow it. Why was he not left there?

Doctor
The patient was transferred to St Ita's because it was considered more suitable for his condition. I regret it is not possible to have him transferred back to St Brendan's Hospital.

Another Meeting With a Historian

The **Historian** *returns.*

Historian   I know you can't use PowerPoint in a play, but you need to get your head around these.

She starts a slideshow.

These figures were compiled by Doctor Damien Brennan of of Trinity College Dublin. These are the numbers of people per thousand in psychiatric hospitals in England and Wales in 1889:

She clicks. The numbers in square brackets appear on the slide but are not spoken. [260]

and 1955.

Click. [534]

And these are the numbers in Scotland. 1889:

Click. [254]

and 1955.

Click. [615]

Very similar.

And these are the numbers in Ireland. 1889.

Click. [452]

1955.

Click. [1082]

They're almost literally off the chart.

She lets this sinks in. Click: new slide.

This is the number of psychiatric beds per 100,000 population in 1955, according to the World Health Organisation. Let's start with another small European country – Finland.

Click.

Two hundred and fifty-six.

Our neighbours: England and Wales?

Click.

Three hundred and fifty-seven.

And Scotland?

Click.

Four hundred and thirty-six.

Northern Ireland:

Click.

Four hundred and forty.

What about the USA?

Click.

Five hundred and eleven.

And the Soviet Union – this is just after the death of Stalin, around about the peak of the gulags.

Click.

Six hundred and seventeen.

And Ireland . . .

Click.

Seven hundred and ten. The highest in the world.

She turns off the slides.

You've heard about the Magdalene Laundries and the mother and child homes and the industrial schools. All of that. In the entire history of the Magdalene Laundries, about 10,000 women went through them. On any *one* night in the mid-1950s there were more than double that in our mental hospitals. The mental hospital system was – by far – the largest form of institutional intervention ever to have existed in this country . . . Proportionately it was the largest such system in the *world* . . .

Beat.

I'll leave that with you.

She starts to leave.

Student   But why?

The **Historian** *stops.*

Student   Why did we lock all these people up?

Historian   Why don't you dig into it a bit more and see what you come up with?

'Degeneracy in the Stock'
Cousin in Dublin
Dear Sir,
My cousin was a patient of yours for a time and I was obliged to declare this as part of my application to study to become a priest at All Hallows college. I was rejected on the grounds that there was mental illness in the family. Could you provide me with a certificate confirming that there were no hereditary factors in his illness?

Mother in Wexford St
I would be much obliged if I could have a certificate about my daughter to verify that the nervous breakdown which she got when she was 14 was due to the operation which she had. My eldest daughter is about to become a nun and she must have this certificate for the Order at her next interview.

Children's Home in Dun Laoghaire
A child under my care here in the home is up for adoption. He had an uncle who was in Grangegorman Mental Hospital. The Adoption Committee have asked me to write to you for an opinion as to whether there was anything in his uncle's history which might prejudice this child's adoption.

Brother in Scotland
My sister could speak and write the following: Latin, Gaelic, English, French and Spanish, quite fluently. She

was treated at your hospital for a number of years until a lobotomy was performed on her. I require a medical statement that her trouble was not a trait in our family – that to the best of your belief her trouble was brought on by study.

The **Doctor** *now provides a reply which serves for all of the above – a reply which manages to be both offensive and reassuring.*

Doctor

All one can say is that the fact that a family member suffered from Schizophrenia does suggest a possible strain of degeneracy in the stock but if it was quite certain that all the other stock was healthy then it is very unlikely that another individual would suffer a hereditary degenerative tendency.

Brother in Meath

Dear Sir,

Please forgive this intrusion, but I am deeply anxious about my sister, who plans to marry an ex-patient of your home early in August. We know definitely that he was in Grangegorman on one occasion. Rumours as to his having been mentally ill on other occasions are causing us untold worry. I would be deeply grateful for any information you could give me.

Doctor (*intemperate*)

Sir,

It is not permitted, even in confidence, to disclose information concerning the illness of any patient treated in this hospital without the written consent of that patient.

Priest in Dublin

Dear Doctor,

A friend of mine is anxious to marry but only recently her fiancé disclosed to her that he spent nine months in Grangegorman about 1940, having been sent there by his doctor.

*The **Doctor** reacts with exasperation, anticipating the same request as before.*

Priest in Dublin
This has made my friend anxious in case there should be any likelihood of a recurrence of his trouble. Could I ask your confidential advice on the matter, as she wants me to direct her as to what she should do.

Doctor (*dictating, impatient*)
It is not permitted / even in confidence

Secretary   Eh, Doctor – did you see the address?

She shows him the letter.

Doctor   Ah.

He looks at the file in order to prepare his response.

Doctor (*dictating*)
Dear Father,
In the particular case you mention, it is fifteen years since he was in this hospital and it would be advisable to have an up-to-date examination with a fairly complete history of his behaviour. I would suggest that your friend should ask her fiancé to have himself examined and get a clean bill of mental health.

Any further help or information which you require, I shall be only too pleased to give you.

'Over-Religious'

*A **Student** has been collecting various religious artefacts and documents from the boxes.*

Student One   So many rosary beads . . . Miraculous medals . . . Crosses . . .

Patients emerge, fingering beads, for a decade of the Rosary.

Rosary Leader   First Sorrowful Mystery: The Agony in the Garden.

The Rosary continues with an Our Father followed by ten Hail Marys, concluding with the Glory Be. One of the patients leads; the others respond in chorus. This should continue, low, as a background to the scene.

Rosary Leader
  Our Father, who art in heaven, hallowed be thy name. Thy kingdom come, thy will be done, on earth, as it is in heaven.

Chorus
  Give us this day our daily bread and forgive us our trespasses as we forgive those who trespass against us; and lead us not into temptation, but deliver us from evil.

Rosary Leader
  Hail Mary, full of grace, the Lord is with thee. Blessed art thou among women, and blessed is the fruit of thy womb, Jesus.

Chorus
  Holy Mary, Mother of God, pray for us sinners now, and at the hour of our death.

The Hail Marys continue.

Student One   Has anyone read any of these?

Student Two   What?

Student One (*looking through them*)   Prayer cards . . . Pamphlets.

Prayer to Our Lady of Lourdes
  Oh ever immaculate Virgin, Mother of Mercy, Health of the Sick, Refuge of Sinners, Comfortess of the Afflicted, I come to implore your maternal intercession.

Student One (*finding another*)   Little prayer books . . .

Prayer to Jesus Crucified
  My Beloved Master, by Thy hands fastened to the Cross, I

beseech Thee wipe away all the sins that my criminal hands have committed.

Student Three   Why would you *read* it?

Student One (*shrugs*)   It was important. To them.

Jesus
(*Matthew 21.22*)
Whatever you ask for in prayer, believing, you shall receive.

Student Four   It's just superstition.

Student One   Take it seriously. These people did.

Student Three (*trying it out – reading a book cover*)   'Devotion to Christ's Sacred Wounds. As said to have been revealed to his servant, Sister Mary Martha Chambon.'

Sister Mary Martha (*prostrating herself*)
Lord – the redeeming Blood – it pours out in torrents from your adorable Wounds.

Jesus
I alone can shed this divine Blood. I am your Spouse and your Father. I give Myself utterly to you for the salvation of souls. Are you vowed to Me?

Sister Mary Martha
Yes, Lord.

Jesus
Then you should be nailed to the Cross with Me.

Student Three   This is some weird shit.

Student Five   You can take it seriously without taking it literally.

The Lord
(*Isaias 49.15*)
Can a woman forget her infant? And if she should forget, yet will I not forget thee.

Priest in Cavan

Dear Doctor,

I should be very grateful if you would kindly let me have your esteemed opinion of my sister's present condition. I have called a number of times to see and I found her in very good spirits, but still over-religious.

The Rosary, which has continued all the while, concludes:

Rosary Leader

Glory be to the Father, and to the Son, and to the Holy Spirit.

Chorus

As it was in the beginning, is now, and ever shall be, world without end. Amen.

Meeting Mick

Mick *emerges. He exists in a different time and space to the other characters. He is similar to the* **Historian**, *in that he is contemporary, but he is not consciously addressing the* **Students**. *He is similar to the letter-writers, in that he is of this world of the hospital, but he is not a manifestation of the archives.*

Mick   I was always at home with the word of Jesus . . . I used to find I could connect much more deeply with people by remaining in a certain state – I can only call it a state of inner stillness. I was trying to find the answers more through my gut than through my head.

I would . . . stand . . . in places around the city . . .

Sometimes I was arrested. For 'loitering'. But people got used to me. I won't say my behaviour was 'average' . . . For my family, it wasn't the most positive engagement their son could have with life . . . But that's where I was at.

Warming to his audience.

On one occasion – I'll be fully frank with you – I think I read it in the Bible somewhere that a prophet walked through a village naked as a way of drawing attention to his message . . . I cannot see anything wrong with the human body and I cannot see anything wrong with it being exposed . . . This is the most extreme behaviour that I ever consciously did . . . I know I had no clothes on inside the house, and then I remember going out the door, presuming they'd stop me –

Mother (*calling from the kitchen*)   You going out, Michael? Be back for dinner.

Mick   I remember walking along the driveway and coming to the gate, and

A **Woman** *and* **Child** *come along the street towards* **Mick**.

Mick   some people were coming along the street, and this woman

Woman *stops and screams*.

Mick   was quite shocked.

Later on, I met the same lady coming down the street. I said,

(*To* **Woman**.) I'm sorry if I frighted you. But why would that be?

Woman   You frightened the child.

Mick   Ah. Fair enough.

'That's a good enough reason to wear clothes – to not frighten children,' I thought.

I remember talking to the mother of a lad I knew, and she said

Friend's Mother   Well, Mick, why did you do it?

Mick   I felt like doing it.

Friend's Mother   Well, you couldn't please a better fellow.

Mick   I remember talking to another neighbour and he said

Neighbour   Sure I walk around with nothing on here in the house.

Mick   It was very releasing . . . But it upset my parents. The police were called, they went up to the bedroom, took down some clothes and said

Garda   Would you ever put them on?

Mick   If you're *telling* me to put them on, I won't . . . I don't feel it's the natural thing to do right now.

Garda   For Jaysus' sake, *please* will you put them on?

Mick   When people *ask* you it's very different to when they *tell* you.

Claire Keeley's Story – 1908–1914

*A **Man** and a **Woman** drink tea at an unset table. They are chatting and laughing, low. They share a loaf of bread, with butter and jam. **Claire**, in her room, watches them while trying not to attract their attention.*

*The **Nurse** arrives, leading the **Doctor**.*

Title: December 19, 1908

Doctor   And this is . . .

Nurse   New admission. 19308. Keeley –

Claire (*conspiratorial*)   These people –

Nurse   Mrs Claire Keeley.

Doctor (*reading file*)   'Delusional insanity.'

Claire   They undermined me.

Man   And it worked.

Doctor   How did they undermine you, Mrs Keeley?

Claire   They held their meetings next door.

Woman   That's her gone now, anyway.

Claire   They *talked* about me.

Man   The street can breathe easy.

Claire   They *are* talking about me!

Doctor   What did they say?

Woman   The hussy!

Claire   A revolver! They talked about a revolver.

The **Man** *and* **Woman** *laugh.*

A new **Doctor** *and* **Nurse** *arrive, seamlessly taking the place of the previous pair, without any interruption in the rhythm.*

Title: January 19, 1909

Man   We won't need to take matters into our own hands, now.

Doctor (*looking over the notes*)   Tell me about the revolver, Mrs Keeley. Did *you* have a revolver?

Woman   We can let the children out on the street again.

Doctor   It says here you threatened to shoot someone, Mrs Keeley.

Claire   There was a lot of low work going on.

Doctor   What do you mean by 'low work', Mrs Keeley?

Woman   Three children by different men . . .

Claire   Scandal.

Man   And none of them her husband.

Claire   Dreadful scandal.

Doctor   How is her diet?

Man   It's the husband I pity.

Nurse   She's refusing her meals, Doctor.

Man   He'll never live down the shame.

Doctor   Is there anything wrong with the food, Mrs Keeley?

Claire   Why do you think I didn't eat it?

Woman   It's a wonder the husband didn't get rid of her sooner.

Doctor   Mrs Keeley, you need to eat. To get well.

Claire   That's not what I'm here for.

*The **Man** and **Woman** get up to leave, laughing, leaving a mess behind.*

*A new **Doctor** and **Nurse** arrive, taking the place of the previous pair.*

Title: June 19, 1909

Laughter from off.

Doctor   *What* are you here for, Mrs Keeley?

Claire   To watch them, of course.

Doctor   Where are 'they', Mrs Keeley?

Claire   Outside. They're outside.

Woman (*from off*)   The hussy.

Claire   I can hear them.

Doctor (*glancing back at notes*)   How is her weight, Nurse?

Nurse   Stable, Doctor.

*An **Orderly** arrives at the table, and proceeds to place the left-overs on a plate on a tray – as if for giving to someone else.*

Doctor   Appetite?

Nurse   Good.

Claire (*to the **Orderly***)   It's not clean!

Doctor   What's wrong with it, Mrs Keeley?

Claire   It is not what I am used to.

Doctor   You get exactly the same as everyone else gets.

Claire   But I am not 'everyone'.

A new **Doctor** *and* **Nurse** *arrive, taking the place of the previous pair.*

Title: January 19, 1910

Doctor   So who are you, then?

Claire   I am Claire O'Connell Walsh Bellew Keeley.

A **Waiter** *has appeared, and taken the tray from the* **Orderly**. *The* **Waiter** *proceeds to lay the table properly, and place the left-overs at it.*

Doctor   And who am *I*, Mrs Keeley?

Claire   How should I know you? We have never met.

Doctor   We have met a number of times, Mrs Keeley.

Claire (*to* **Waiter**)   This is a poor show for the County Inn.

Doctor   This is not the County Inn, Mrs Keeley. This is the Richmond Asylum.

A new **Doctor** *and* **Nurse** *arrive, taking the place of the previous pair.*

Title: January 19, 1911

Claire   We have horses and fowl at home. I will send for butter and eggs.

The **Waiter** *leaves, offended.*

Doctor   So why are you here, Mrs Keeley?

Claire   I came in to keep an eye on those people. But I am here long enough to go home. And the food is not clean.

Doctor   How is her appetite?

Nurse   Reasonable.

Doctor   Sleep?

Nurse   She sleeps well.

Title: January 19, 1912

The **Doctor** *and* **Nurse** *no longer change over.*

Doctor   Is she still hearing voices?

Claire   Don't you hear what they are saying?

Nurse   They come and go, Doctor.

A peal of laughter from off.

Claire   I'm going home this evening.

Title: January 19, 1913

Claire   My business here is over.

Doctor   What business is that, Mrs Keeley?

Claire   Watching. I had to watch them. With their low work. But it is time to go home.

A **Royal Attendant** *arrives.*

Doctor   Does she receive visitors?

Claire   I need a new dress to go home in.

Nurse   Not that I'm aware of, Doctor.

The **Attendant** *leaves to find one.*

Title: January 19, 1914

Claire   The Queen ordered a new dress. It should have arrived.

Doctor (*to the* **Nurse**)   The Queen?

Nurse   So she says, Doctor.

Claire   You *know* I am of royal blood.

Title: January 19, 1915

The **Attendant** *returns, perhaps carrying a wrap or scarf, which is handed to* **Claire** *with a bow.*

Claire   I am Queen Claire Keeley Victoria.

The **Attendant** *lights a candle on the table.*

Doctor   What has you here, in that case?

Claire   Why, this is one of my palaces. But I will not be here much longer. I am going home.

She may wrap the item around her.

Title: January 19, 1915

Doctor   That is a very elegant scarf, Mrs Keeley. Very appropriate.

Claire   I am Queen Victoria.

Doctor   And where are we, Mrs Keeley? What is the name of this house?

Claire   I am here in my own place. I am the Queen of England. This is my home.

The **Attendant** *snuffs out the candle.*

'Home'

Mother in Crumlin

Dear Doctor,

My daughter was home on thirty days' trial from St Brendan's. She was on her third week and we were delighted to have her home for Christmas – but do you know what she done on Tuesday 22 December? She went into town, met some fellow home on holidays from England, went into a lounge bar and he gave her a dose of whiskey. This carry on will have to stop – I am not able for any more trouble with her. I am only too glad to take my daughter home but I am leaving it to you, Doctor, to let me know if she is fit to come home.

Husband in Killarney St

I really want my wife home – I really mean it – but I have got no place to take her home to. My wife's mother closed the house – she will not have my wife in the house as her married son is taking it over.

Mother in Blackrock

About three years ago, my son had a mental breakdown and spent about eleven months in your hospital. On discharge – cured – he came home and resumed his job teaching in the Vocational School. Some time ago, I noticed that he was buying books, wholesale, on poetry and art, and applying himself over-enthusiastically to painting and writing poems.

He propounded the idea very firmly that there is no hell and proceeded to support the contention by readings from the Bible.

He is firmly convinced that his health is perfect and indeed it appears to be physically, although he has for nearly a year given up meat-eating.

I shall be very thankful if you will look up his hospital record and give me any advice you may think useful together with an indication of the possibility of care.

PS I forgot to say he is a regular and confirmed picture-goer.

Mother in Dalkey

Dear Doctor,
I enclose a letter I received from my daughter for your kind attention.

Daughter

Dear Mam,
Many thanks for sending in the sponge cake and the scones for my birthday.

Also thank Tim for his card and Anthony for his letter.

There is nothing I want in here at the moment. My clothes are folded away and I am using the house clothes as my own clothes would only get lost in the laundry. I would be glad to have my sandals in as the boots are too heavy at present.

Mother in Dalkey

In view of what she says in the third paragraph, I would like to have your report on her.

Daughter

I know it's for the doctors to decide what to do. Well, as far as I know, they want to see us out of here and at home and are waiting to hear from your end.

Mother in Dalkey

We are most anxious to have her at home – if we thought she would be cooperative and would not get a relapse. However, being an only girl, she might get lonely.

Daughter

If you don't want me to be at home please say so as we can then make other arrangements.

Mother in Dalkey

I think if it is possible that you could arrange to place her under supervision elsewhere, where she could have a job, it would be better in her case.

Daughter

The weather is very changeable here. I suppose the chickens take up a good bit of time, they are always delicate at first.

Mother in Dalkey

She would be always welcome at home in her spare time and holidays.

Daughter

All the news for now.

With best wishes and love.

Mother in Dalkey

I would be most thankful for your advice.

Doctor

Your daughter had improved fairly well on a course of Serpasil treatment but relapsed quickly after the completion of the course and was troublesome, impulsive and deluded. She has been recommended another course of Serpasil therapy and is now quieter in behaviour and more cooperative – but she is far from being fit for discharge at present.

Claire Keeley's Story – 1916

An **Orderly** *arrives at a hall door.*

Orderly Mr Keeley – I have a message from the Richmond Asylum. I regret to have to inform you that your wife Claire Keeley is dangerously ill.

Resident Eh, Keeley?

Orderly Thomas Keeley? This is number 33, Lower Bridge Street?

Resident (*remembering*) Ah yeh – a Keeley lived here, that's right. But he's gone about two years, with the family.

Orderly Have you an address for him?

Resident No, he didn't leave one. I think he may have gone foreign.

'Gone Foreign'

Sister in Birmingham

Dearest sister,

I know life in hospital is a bit lonely at times, but please God you will be home soon. I hope the insulin treatment has made an improvement and besides the rest will do you good, as you have had a strenuous time between work and

study. I am still working at Boots, toiling away. I was glad
to see you have been able to get to Croke Park during the
season. We listen to it on the radio here.

Daughter in Lancashire

Dear Mam,

Just a few lines hoping you are keeping well as I am
myself. Well Mam we are sending Jimmy new pants and
shoes and socks. I hope he will take care of them. Well
Mam I am looking forward to when you are coming
home. Well Mam we are having lovely weather now here
in Lancashire. I hope it keeps up like that. Well Mam I will
be looking forward to hearing from you soon.

Mother in Liverpool

Dear Sir,

I received a letter from my daughter from which I gather
she is a patient at your hospital. Would you be so kind as
to let me know what is wrong with her and how she came
to be there? I have had no word from her granny, my
mother. I have been in England this seventeen years and it
is little I know about her. If you will just let me know how
bad she is, I will be very grateful.

Wife in Liverpool

Dear Doctor,

How I come to be over here in Liverpool is my husband
and myself agreed to give up our house as we could not
carry on any longer. We made up our minds to come over
to England to take a job as caretakers. When we had all
fixed to leave our house my husband did not feel at all
well. So he said I could come over and wait until he got
better. I could not take my two children as I had no place
to come to so I took my son and put Ann our little girl into
the Birds Nest home in Dun Laoghaire. This made
trouble with the Catholic Rescue Society and since then
my husband won't answer my letters. Will you please let
me know how he is getting on.

Claire's Sister

Dear Sir,

Will you kindly let me know when it will be convenient for me to come and see a patient whom I am informed is at the Richmond Mental Hospital. Her name is Mrs Claire Keeley. I am her youngest sister and as far as I can learn her nearest living relative in this country. This is my first visit to Ireland for thirty-five years, since 1899. Can you, therefore, imagine my grief on learning this sad news. She was such a dear lovely girl when we were all young together.

Thanking you in anticipation.

The Board of Governors – 1818–1938

Title: 1818

General chat as the **Governors** *gather.*

Chairman   Good morning, gentlemen. I call this meeting of the Board of Governors of the Richmond Lunatic Asylum to order.

They come to order.

The first item on today's agenda is the question of treatment. Doctor, would you be so good as to give us a report on progress in this regard?

Doctor   Thank you, sir. I am grateful to report that we have had some positive results by use of the circulating swing.

Governor One   The circulating swing? Do elaborate.

Doctor   Of course. I have an illustration here.

It is projected.

This is the very latest design, developed by our colleague in Cork, Doctor Hallaran. He has constructed an apparatus in which up to four persons can be secured at once, seated or horizontal, and be rotated at a speed of one hundred times per minute.

We have found it very effective in dealing with excessive obstinacy.

Governor One   Yes?

Doctor   Yes. We find that after a good go in the swing, patients are usually rather less obstinate.

Governor Three   Oh, very good.

Governor One   And with patients of a more melancholic disposition?

Doctor   It appears to generate a natural interest in the affairs of life . . . Another effect is that it may induce vomiting and evacuation of the bowels, which of course can be highly therapeutic.

Board Members   Of course, of course.

They swap places or swap out with other actors.

Title: 1926

The malaria therapy may be illustrated with slides or performed on a patient in a parallel scene.

Chairman   Ah, gentlemen, may I call this meeting to order? Doctor – you have news of some new therapy.

Doctor   Indeed, Chairman. Malaria therapy.

Governor One   But malaria's a tropical disease – there is no malaria in Ireland.

Doctor   Yes, that is one of the complications. However, we are working hard to introduce it.

Governor One   Ah.

Doctor   Our colleagues on the continent have had prodigious success in treating general paralysis of the insane by causing the patient to be infected with malaria. In fighting the malarial fever, the body also fights off the advanced syphilis infection that causes the insanity.

Governor Three   Extraordinary.

Governor Two   So you induce a mosquito to bite the patient?

Doctor   That was the original idea. We had been collecting mosquitos from customs officers in the port – they often find them in shipments from the tropics. But alas, in our rather more temperate climate, the mosquitos grew rather lazy and could not be induced to bite. So now we simply import infected blood serum.

Governor Three   Ah, very good.

Governor One   And what has the clinical record been?

Doctor   Oh, excellent. Of twenty-five patients treated, two were discharged, cured, another six improved greatly, and seven improved slightly.

Governor Two   And the other . . . ten?

Doctor   On five, it appears to have had no effect whatsoever –

Governor Two   Except for having given them malaria.

Doctor   Quite. And the other five died. Of course, they may have died anyway.

Board Members   Of course.

Chairman   That sounds worth pursuing. I trust you will be continuing to expand the treatment.

Doctor   Yes, absolutely.

They swap places or swap out with other actors.

Title: 1938

The insulin therapy is performed on a patient, in parallel.

Chairman   Gentlemen, the next item on the agenda is a report on this new insulin treatment. Doctor.

Doctor   Thank you, Chairman. Our colleague in Austria, Doctor Manfred Sakel, observed that coma could bring about recovey in patients with general paralysis of the insane. So he has developed a method of deliberately inducing coma, which we have adopted here. This we do by injecting patients with high doses of insulin.

Governor One   And to bring the patient *out* of coma?

Doctor   We administer glucose.

Governor Three   And the patient is then cured?

Doctor   Well, the effects are not necessarily quite so dramatic.

Governor Two   This is a one-off treatment?

Doctor   No. We put the patient in a coma daily.

Governor Two   For how many days?

Doctor   Oh, fifty or sixty, or so.

Governor One   And what are the clinical results like?

Doctor   Oh, very good. Though there have been some complications, of course.

Board Members   Of course.

Governor Two   Such as?

Doctor   Obesity is common. Convulsions. Brain damage can be a regrettable side effect.

Chairman   Well let's keep an eye on that, shall we? But I think we're all agreed – we should expand our use of this new treatment.

'Just an Ordinary Sickness'

The patient who has just received the insulin treatment now corresponds with the hospital.

Former Patient

Dear Doctor,

Insulin treatment has occupied my mind periodically ever since I got it during a period of about six weeks under your supervision, some ten or eleven years ago. It occurs to me that I might benefit by insulin again. But first I wish to know why I first got it. How serious was the necessity of insulin treatment in my case?

Doctor

Dear Sir,

The insulin treatment which you received was not for any physical complaint but for the mental illness from which you were suffering. It would be most inadvisable that you should take insulin or another drug without medical advice and prescription.

Former Patient

Doctor,

My illness may have had elements of a mental illness, but I'd say it was also an economic one – and a question of whether I was ever to get anywhere, at home. To simply declare a person mentally unbalanced and confine him to hospital was not a total handling of the situation. As it turned out, I had to go to England to work, and the jobs I had were never any good. I regret to have to say, Doctor, that if your way of working cured me in one small respect, it spoiled my life from other angles of view – and such happens to lots of Irish people. While Ireland isn't rich, quite a few inside the country have considerable incomes – particularly yourself – and I've no doubt but that you and several others owe me quite a lot of money directly, if the matter were thrashed out.

Doctor (*to* **Secretary**)   Can't say I like his tone. Best not to indulge it with a reply.

They move on with their correspondence.

Meanwhile, two American **Consular Officials** *enter the space with the* **Former Patient**.

Former Patient
Dear Doctor,
Yet one more from me.

Consular Official One   We just have a few questions.

Consular Official Two   Shan't detain you unnecessarily.

Former Patient
This time it's urgent. I want to know *what* must I say when asked such questions as

Consular Official One   Have you ever had any mental illness?

Former Patient (*hesitant*)   Eh . . .

Consular Official Two   Has there ever been insanity in your family?

Former Patient (*alarmed*)   Ah!

Consular Official One   A 'Yes' or 'No' will suffice.

Former Patient
What a mess I'd be in if I say 'No' and the authorities in question find out that the answer is 'Yes'.

Consular Official Two   It is a straightforward question.

Former Patient
The American consular authorities, to be precise . . .

Consular Official One   Sir, under the Immigration and Nationality Act, 'people having physical or mental defects' are excludable aliens.

Former Patient
I'd make better progress altogether in the USA. However, everything has to be 'alright'.

Consular Official Two   Sir, you should know: we have a highly-developed fact-finding operation . . .

Consular Official One (*making phone call*)   Is that the Dublin embassy? We need you to investigate an immigration case . . . (*Continues sotto voce.*)

Former Patient

I'd possibly be found out to be a liar if I said 'No' . . .

Consular Official One (*into phone*)   . . . Yes, use *all* your intelligence sources.

Former Patient (*alarmed*)

. . . but I don't reckon it's at all justice to myself to say an unqualified 'Yes' . . .

Consular Official Two   So, let's go over this again: Have you ever had any mental illness?

Former Patient

It was just an ordinary sickness that could have been mended by a proper diet on a good holiday . . . if I could have afforded it.

Consular Official One   Has there ever been insanity in your family?

Former Patient

I know of no reason to suspect anything queer about my ancestors, except that they were ordinary people and don't figure among the respected and influential.

Please, Doctor, send me a statement specifically explaining the illness in question and all about it.

The **Doctor** *sighs and prepares to respond.*

Doctor

When you were admitted to this hospital, you were suffering from an inability to reason properly about matters. It appears that you had failed in your first Arts examination and that your behaviour generally indicated that you were suffering from illness of your mind. The nature of these symptoms were in favour of a diagnosis of

Schizophrenia. You received deep insulin treatment and appeared to improve. It appears to me from your letter that you have regained full mental health, of which I am very glad.

The **Former Patient** *acknowledges the compliment.*

Doctor
With regard to your query as to how you should answer questions addressed to you by consular authorities . . .

Kafka-like, the ritual with the **Officials** *begins again.*

Consular Official One   We just have a few questions.

Consular Official Two   Shan't detain you unnecessarily.

Doctor
I could not give you any advice on such a matter. That is something you must decide for yourself.

Consular Official One   Have you ever had any mental illness?

Consular Official Two   Has there ever been insanity in your family?

Doctor   I do feel, however, that any indication to the immigrant authorities would result in your being rejected as an immigrant citizen.

The **Former Patient** *is left, undecided, confronting the* **Officials**.

Claire Keeley's Story – 1920s

This scene consists of five separate interactions, which start sequentially and then continue simultaneously.

First Interaction

A **Nurse** *brings* **Claire** *to meet the* **Doctor**.

Nurse   Claire Keeley for her six-monthly assessment, Doctor.

Doctor   Number?

Nurse   19308.

Doctor   How are you, Mrs Keeley?

Claire   You should speak when you're spoken to, young man.

Doctor   Plenty of spirit, clearly.

Nurse   She has . . . exalted ideas, Doctor. When she's coherent. Quiet otherwise.

This interaction continues, inaudible (or indistinct), while, elsewhere on stage, the scene replicates: another **Nurse** *brings another* **Claire** *to meet another* **Doctor**.

Second Interaction

This **Claire** *is shrunken into herself, mumbling.*

Doctor   Patient?

Nurse   19308, Claire Keeley.

Doctor   And?

Nurse   Dull and confused.

Doctor   So no change, then.

Nurse   When we can make her out at all, she believes she's a queen.

The interaction continues. Elsewhere, the **Lady of the Bedchamber** *brings* **Queen Claire** *to meet the* **Physician to the Queen**.

Third Interaction

Physician to the Queen (*bowing*)   Your Majesty.

Lady of the Bedchamber   Thank you for your patience, my Lord.

Physician to the Queen   It is ever rewarded by her Majesty's presence. I trust the food is to your liking, Your Majesty?

Queen Claire   Is it from the palace garden?

Physician to the Queen   Of course.

Queen Claire   It is rather predictable. Let us eat game.

Physician to the Queen   Lady of the Bedchamber, is Her Majesty comfortable at night?

The interaction continues. Elsewhere, another **Nurse** *brings another* **Claire** *to meet another* **Doctor**.

Fourth Interaction

This **Claire** *resists the* **Nurse**'s *attempts to lead her, and has to be restrained by an* **Orderly**.

Nurse   Claire Keeley, 19308.

Doctor   Resistive, clearly.

Nurse   Yes. Noisy, abusive, destructive.

The interaction continues. When **Claire** *realises she can't get away, she tears at her clothing. Elsewhere:*

Fifth Interaction

This **Claire** *is utterly docile.*

Nurse   19308, Doctor. Claire Keeley. Very quiet.

The interaction continues. The volume and tension mount. The culumative effect is a cacophany.

Then: **Ophelia** *enters, singing softly to herself, carrying flowers.*

Ophelia
They bore him barefaced on the bier;
And in his grave rained many a tear.

She arrives at one of the interactions, where **Claire** *is upset or confused.*

Ophelia (*to* **Claire**)
There's rosemary, that's for remembrance – pray you, love, remember.

Claire *takes the rosemary, and leaves, followed by the* **Doctor** *and* **Nurse**. **Ophelia** *moves on to the next interaction.*

Ophelia (*to* **Claire**)
And there is pansies, that's for thoughts.

They leave. **Ophelia** *moves on.*

Ophelia (*to the* **Nurse**)
There's fennel for you, (*to the* **Doctor**) and columbines.

They leave. **Ophelia** *moves on.*

Ophelia (*to* **Claire**)
There's rue for you. And here's some for me. We may call it herb of grace o' Sundays. O you must wear your rue with a difference.

They leave. **Ophelia** *moves on.*

Ophelia (*to* **Claire**)
There's a daisy. I would give you some violets, but they withered all when my father died. They say he made a good end –

Another **Doctor** *and* **Nurse** *watch this. All the previous groups have left the scene. The* **Nurse** *approaches* **Ophelia**.

Nurse   Claire –

Ophelia (*singing, to herself*)
For bonny sweet Robin is all my joy.
And will he not come again?
And will he not come again?
No, no, he is dead:
Go to thy death-bed,
He never will come again.

Nurse   Let's go back to bed, Claire.

Claire's *song continues under their conversation.*

Ophelia
His beard was as white as snow,
All flaxen was his poll.
He is gone, he is gone,
And we cast away moan:
God ha' mercy on his soul!

Doctor   A document in madness . . .

(*Assessing her.*) Seems calm, though.

Any family contact at all?

Nurse   The husband's dead. I think the children are in England.

Ophelia
And of all Christian souls, I pray God. God be with ye.

Nurse   That's it, Claire. Come on now.

Meeting With a Psychiatrist

The **Teacher** *leads the psychiatrist, Professor* **Brendan Kelly**, *in.*

Teacher   I thought we could all do with talking to a psychiatrist –

Student One   A generic psychiatrist?

Teacher   No, this is Brendan Kelly, Professor of Psychiatry at Trinity College Dublin – Professor, maybe to start with, what can you tell from the Case Book entries about Claire Keeley's condition?

Brendan Kelly   Well, it does it does seem relatively clear, even from this distance, that she had some . . . unusual ideas – maybe delusions . . . There's a *reasonable* chance she was what we would now call mentally ill. Of course as time goes on, her ideas about her being the Queen seem to become a little more focused and some of that is likely the result of being in the impoverished environment of the institution for so long.

Student Two   Do you mean, like, a coping mechanism of some sort?

Brendan Kelly   Yes – in the absence of other stimuli, these ideas become clearer.

Student Three   So how would you diagnose her?

Brendan Kelly   Well, look, we probably shouldn't apply the diagnostic systems and thinking of today to this report of symptoms of more than 100 years ago . . . But if we *were* to . . . Well, somebody with this kind of initial symptoms – a year and eight months after the birth of a child – tentatively, you'd say a post-partum psychosis.

But it seems to have persisted for a long time . . . Delusions that persist for that long, and the hearing of voices – that comes and goes in the notes, it's not terribly convincing – but if that *was* there it does look more like schizophrenia.

Student Four   And how would you treat her for that?

Brendan Kelly   Today?

Student Four   Yes.

Brendan Kelly   If she arrived in today, with her husband, with this story of the argument with the neighbour and let's say a delusion that there were indeed people from Australia in her home, and she has a one-year-eight-month-old baby, we would do a risk evaluation: we'd see were there any delusions or thoughts regarding the baby that led to a risk to it. If there weren't, we would not admit her to hospital.

We'd almost certainly prescribe an antipsychotic medication – but these were not available until the 1950s.

Student Five   So what kind of treatment would she have got, during the decades she was here?

Brendan Kelly   There's no mention at all in her entries in the Case Book of treatment. Though they didn't always record it in the Case Book.

The first physical treatment introduced here during this period was malaria therapy in the 1920s. But that was for general paralysis of the insane, and she didn't have that. The next possibility would have been insulin coma therapy but that was introduced here in 1938, and she would have been at a very advanced stage then, so they wouldn't have given her treatment. So, no, there was no treatment here.

The thing about Ireland is this was very commonly the case. We didn't take to these biological treatments in Ireland with the same enthusiasm that they did in other countries.

A **Student** *raises their hand – the same student who asked the 'why' question previously.*

Brendan Kelly   Our emphasis in Ireland was always on institutionalisation – it was always on admission and keeping people in the institution.

Student   Yes, but *why?*

Brendan Kelly   Have you talked to any historians? I think that might be a question for them.

'This Wild Wife of Mine'

Teacher (*handing out copies of a letter*)   OK everybody, this is a difficult one. I wanted to wait till we were further into the research process before we tackled it.

They choose one of the men.

Will you start it off – just read it – and the rest of you: be ready to put it on the floor, as we discussed.

The **Student** *takes the letter and begins reading.*

Husband
    Dear Sir,

I beg to write you with a view to help in treatment for my wife.

Her language lately is very smutty and obscene –

Student Actress (*to herself*)   'Smutty' – what the fuck is smutty.

Husband

that is when she speaks at all – mostly she is in a cross, morose mood.

She has made several violent attacks on me with weapons such as bite hooks, sticks, stones, iron bars, sometimes hurting and cutting my head and face. My father is a weak old man of 86 years of age. While I was away from home one night this wild wife of mine went into his room, abused him, jeered, lifted up her dress and was performing queer antics.

Teacher   OK.

He calls on the first pair.

Remember: make strong choices. Commit.

This sequence should be played with the rhythm of improv, as the actors stutter from one line to the next as they find their way to the next thought.

Wife   Cunt.

There is a frisson while the class assesses this – is it allowed? Has she gone too far?

Husband (*urgently*)   Don't say that.

Wife   Cunt.

Pause.

That's what you want, isn't it?

Husband (*reaching out to her*)   Please don't say that –

Wife   Don't touch me!

Husband   I just want you back –

Wife   Back? Back from where?

Husband   Back to yourself.

Wife   Some day I'll have you behind iron bars and I will get in a man that I would like. A man that can please me.

Husband   Please, love / why do you say those things

Wife   I'm not your 'love'. There was never any love in this house.

Husband   You cannot mean that – you cannot say it –

Wife   Don't tell me what I can and can't say!

Teacher (*quietly*)   Change.

The second pair steps into the scene, seamlessly.

The stakes rise.

Husband   You have to get help, / you have to let me –

Wife   There is no help / for this, we're beyond

Husband   I talked to the parish priest, he said / there could be support available

Wife   The priest? You talked to the priest / about me?

Husband   We need help . . . from / somewhere.

Wife   If he lays a fucking finger on me, I'll cut his fucking head off, / so I will.

Husband   I don't understand . . . what's happened / to you?

Wife   What is there to understand? Why do you think / you should be able

Husband   You weren't like this before / we married, you never did anything

Wife   You didn't know me before. Oh you'd have thought my life was fierce quare then, alright – knocking about with my girls . . . and a few fellows from the town, / going to the pictures

Husband (*with dread*)   What do you mean by 'knocking about'?

Wife   Kissing . . . Embracing . . . Mauling each other during the pictures, in the dark . . .

Husband   You're only saying this to / hurt me

Wife   By God but they were men. Real men. With real stiff cocks / that they

Husband   Don't / say that

Wife   that they fucking knew what to do with. / That I knew

Husband   You didn't / do anything

Wife   Oh I did. And I loved it. Why wouldn't I – I was young. And beautiful. And free. Before I – Before I / met you

Husband   You could have gotten pregnant –

(*Suddenly realising.*) Did you – Did you get pregnant?

Wife   We protected against that.

Teacher   Change.

The third pair steps into the scene. The stakes rise.

Husband   Why didn't you tell me this before . . . before I married you?

Wife   Why do you think? You'd have broken it off. What would have been left for me then?

Husband   It would have been better than this. Surely.

Wife   Bad as this is, you don't know what it was like before.

Husband   You lied to me.

Wife   I never promised to be faithful to you.

Husband   You took vows.

Wife   I didn't *believe* the vows.

There is a shift in his tone – more ominous.

Husband   I told the priest and doctor about you.

She screams at him.

Husband   I had to.

Wife   And you wonder why I prefer to sleep with the dogs in the stable, rather than you?

Husband   The work is nearly all done now.

Wife   That's all you care about.

Husband   If you will not agree to have treatment, / whatever treatment

The **Teacher** *cues two of the men, silently. They stand, ready to enter the scene as* **Orderlies**.

Wife   What treatment?

Husband   *Any* treatment – any treatment they suggest / that you need

Wife   *Who* suggests? What are you / talking about?

Husband   Then you must realise / this conduct cannot

Wife (*rising alarm*)   Realise *what*? What have / you done?

Husband   It . . . cannot be tolerated . . . indefinitely.

Wife (*panicking*)   What are you talking about?

The **Orderlies** *enter.*

Wife   What do you mean?

Orderly   Please, now, missus.

Wife   What's going on?

Orderly   We're just here to help.

Wife   What have you done?

They start to restrain her – she resists.

Wife   No!

Husband   Please, love, just do as they say.

Teacher   Change.

The next student steps in as the **Husband**. *His pair as the* **Wife** *is the* **Student Actress** *from earlier. She holds back.*

Husband (*committing to the scene*)   Just do as they say.

Student Actress   I'm not doing it.

The **Orderlies** *go to restrain her. (They think she is playing the scene.)*

Student Actress   I'm not doing it.

Orderly   Please, m'am.

Student Actress   I'm not doing the *scene*.

Husband   What?

Teacher   It's just an exercise.

Student Actress   I won't do it.

Teacher   I said – if anybody finds this material difficult, they can step out / at any time

Student Actress   It's *degrading*.

Teacher   This whole thing was degrading! That's the point. These institutions. We're trying to illuminate that. That brings dignity / to it

Student Actress   You think this is dignified? A bunch of students playing with someone's medical records?

Teacher   This is the *archive*. It is testimony – this is what his letter said. We honour them by learning from it. We have a *responsibility* / to learn from it

Student Actress   *Whose* archive?

Teacher   The hospital's.

Student Actress   Where's *her* voice? Whose voices has this archive given us?

Student One   Doctors'. Nurses'.

Student Actress   Yes!

Student Two   Parents'.

Student One   Husbands'.

Student Actress   Where are the *patients*? Where are the *women*'s voices?

Student Three   Oh *don't* make this all about women *again*!

Student One   She's right!

Husband   This woman is making this man's life a misery. / She's not the vitctim

Student One   How do we *know* that?

Student Actress   Who has the power here?

Student Three   She's intimidating him –

Student Four   She's *violent* towards him –

Student Actress   She's lashing out. But she's powerless.

(*Imitating.*) 'The work is nearly all done now'? Does that sound like she's an equal?

Teacher (*trying to reassert control*)   OK, you raise / very good points

Student Actress   And who *else* has the power, here?

Student One   The Priest.

Student Actress   And the Doctor. What do we know about the power priests and doctors wielded over women in Ireland?

Teacher (*firmly*)   Let's try a different approach. Take all of that *into* the character, and play her / whichever way you want to

Student Actress   I'm not going to 'play' her. We have no access to her.

Husband   That's why we're improvising.

Student Actress   This is not material for an improv game.

Student Four   But it's our job to tell this story –

Student Actress   It's not a 'story'. There's no 'three acts'. There's no resolution here. No 'journey'.

Husband   So what can we *do* with these letters?

Beat.

Student Actress   Just take them for what they are. Fragments. Read them. Talk about them. But don't pretend like we can know who these people were.

Claire Keeley's Story – 1930s

*The **Doctor** and **Nurse** assess **Claire Keeley**'s health, the **Doctor** taking notes. This may take place in her room or in the **Doctor**'s office.*

Title: January 19, 1935

Doctor   And who is this?

Nurse   19308. Mrs Claire Keeley.

Doctor   Hello, Mrs Keeley.

Claire *does not reply audibly. The **Doctor** looks to the **Nurse**.*

Nurse   She's quiet, Doctor. Incoherent when she does speak. Clean but untidy.

*The **Doctor** finishes writing this down.*

Doctor   Thank you. Next patient.

They move on – or the **Nurse** *leads* **Claire** *away.*

Either **Doctor** *or* **Nurse** *swap each time, so there is constant change.*

Title: January 19, 1936

Doctor   Patient?

Nurse   19308. Mrs Claire Keeley.

Doctor   Hello, Mrs Keeley.

Nurse   There's no point, Doctor. She's devoid of sense. Incoherent.

Doctor   Demented?

Nurse   Yes.

Doctor   But quiet?

Nurse   Yes, but not if you interfere with her.

Doctor (*writing*)   . . . resistive if interfered with.

Thank you, Nurse.

A new combination of **Doctor** *and* **Nurse** *assess her.*

Title: January 19, 1938

Doctor   And this is?

Nurse   19308. Mrs Claire Keeley.

Doctor   How is she?

Nurse   No change. Demented. Rarely speaks. When she does, she is incoherent. Untidy.

Doctor   Yes, so I can see. Thank you Nurse.

A new combination of **Doctor** *and* **Nurse** *assess her.*

Title: January 19, 1938

Doctor   Patient?

Nurse   19308. Mrs Claire Keeley.

Doctor   Demented, I see. Any sense to her at all?

Nurse   None, Doctor.

Doctor   Thank you, Nurse.

A new combination of **Doctor** *and* **Nurse** *assess her.*

Title: January 19, 1939.

Doctor   This is patient number . . .

Nurse   19308.

Doctor   Yes. She seems clean – if untidy. Quiet?

Nurse   Mostly. Speaks very little at all.

A new combination of **Doctor** *and* **Nurse** *assess her.*

Title: January 19, 1940.

Doctor   19308?

Nurse   Yes, Doctor.

Doctor   I see she has valvular heart disease. How is she?

Nurse   Quiet, Doctor. Dull. Seldom speaks.

A new combination of **Doctor** *and* **Nurse** *assess her.*

Title: January 19, 1941

For the next interaction, **Claire** *is bedridden. Either the scene takes place at her bed, or they are at her room but she has been moved to medical ward, or the* **Nurse** *is reporting to the* **Doctor** *in his office.*

Doctor   Patient number?

Nurse   19308.

Doctor   Ah yes, Claire Keeley. Recovering from pneumonia. Still bedridden?

Nurse   Yes, Doctor. She's unable to stand. Incontinent.

Doctor   And her manner?

Nurse   Dull and demented, Doctor. Seldom speaks.

Doctor   I'll check in on her later.

'Laughing in Chapel'

Brendan Kelly *returns, with the* **Teacher**.

Teacher   Professor, we have some other patient cases we'd like to ask you about – ones where we can't quite work out what's going on.

He hands over to the **Students**.

Student One   This is a letter from the Medical Superintendent here at Grangegorman to the Reverend Mother at St Anne's School, Kilmacud. He seems to be sending her a report on a girl who had been transferred to the hospital from the school.

Brendan Kelly   St Anne's was a reformatory school – generally the reformatories were for children who had offended in some way – a criminal offence. St Anne's was different – it was for girls who were deemed to be a risk to other children because of the girls' sexual experiences.

Student Two   You mean they were sexually active?

Brendan Kelly   Or had been abused. Or had been raped. And it was the girls who were deemed to be a risk and therefore they were sent to schools like St Anne's. So for example, there was a case in 1954 where an employee at the St Joseph's Girls' Reformatory School in Limerick was discovered to have been a long-standing abuser. And so nine of the girls he abused were transferred to St Anne's.

Student One   This is what the doctor says about her. 'There has been no change in the mental state of this patient. She remains troublesome and uncooperative and refuses to occupy herself.'

Brendan Kelly   That's just a description of disruptive behaviour – likely what landed her in St Anne's in the first place. There's no sign whatsoever that that girl is mentally ill. The incidence of mental illness requiring involuntary hospitalisation in this age group is actually quite low and the behavioural pattern there does not suggest it.

Student One   He continues: 'She needs constant supervision because of her escapist tendencies.'

Brendan Kelly   'Escapist tendencies' – the phraseology there is taking a very understandable desire to escape and turning it into a personality trait. It's medicalising a very normal human desire. Things get described as 'tendencies' when there's a desire to describe them as part of an illness. What this *is* is normal behaviour in an *ab*normal setting.

Student Three   This letter is something similar – another patient history. It's a letter from the Medical Superintendent here to another mental hospital, about a patient who has obviously been transferred there from Grangegorman.

'Dear Sir,
This patient was admitted here as a temporary patient from St Mary Magdalene Asylum, Donnybrook' –

Student Four (*interrupting*)   Was there an asylum in Donnybrook?

Brendan Kelly   That was what was referred to as a Magdalene Laundry.

Student Four   So she came *here* from the laundry, and then she was sent *on* to another hospital.

Brendan Kelly   Yes – this young woman was now moving from institution to institution. Once you create institutions, you find people with institutional 'careers' – they never get out of them.

Student Three   OK. So. 'This patient was admitted here as a temporary patient from St Mary Magdalene Asylum,

Donnybrook, where she was stated to have been destructive, tearing up clothes, always laughing in chapel and keeping other girls awake at night.'

Brendan Kelly   Well what's interesting there is these are all behaviours that are disruptive in residential institutions. None of them, on the face of it, indicate mental illness.

Student Three   'On admission, the girl was facile and admitted to having auditory hallucinations but could not tell what the voices said to her. She was dull, retarded and apathetic.'

Brendan Kelly   So she 'admitted' to hearing voices when there's no one there. That suggests that she had to be pressed on the matter before she said that she heard them. If her manner was 'facile' she might have been saying 'no' and then 'yes' and then 'no' and then 'yes' – this happens quite a lot, particularly when people are moving between institutions: whatever you answer probably doesn't matter – you're moving from institution to institution anyway.

And she could not tell what the voices said to her . . . That's very uncommon, because hallucinations are normally heard with *conviction* – in the same way that delusions or false or paranoid beliefs arrive with extra conviction.

Student Three   It continues: 'She had three applications of modified ECT and became a little brighter, but retained her hallucinations.'

Brendan Kelly   OK, ECT: the T means it was intended to be therapeutic – a cure. C is 'convulsive' – the person has a seizure, an epileptic fit. And the E means it was deliberately triggered by applying a very small electrical current across the brain. She had three separate applications of this. That's interesting. ECT is only used now for severe, life-threatening depression, but it was common then to use it early on in treatment. But even then, *three* applications wasn't an evidence-based way to use it.

Student Five   What does that mean?

Brendan Kelly   It wasn't used for *therapeutic* reasons – to treat a condition. It was being used for control of disruptive behaviour.

Student Three   It continues: 'While here, she was quiet and cooperative and worked in the sewing room.' Is that a medical effect of the ECT – that it made her quieter?

Brendan Kelly   No. What we're seeing here is defeat. An awareness that you can't beat the institution once you're inside it – or, at the very least, that the path out is through cooperating with it. She is yielding to the institution.

Student Three   It finishes: 'Shortly after her admission here, a most objectionable and abusive letter was sent to the patient from her mother and brother in Roscommon, warning her not to attempt to return to home under any circumstances.'

Brendan Kelly   Some of the women or girls who were sent there were sent because their behaviour was deemed to be inappropriate in some way . . . Often, this was sexual behaviour. The Magdalene Laundries were started for prostitutes, and then they moved into young women who had a child out of wedlock – but in their later phase in the twentieth century they lost their association with sex out of wedlock. We don't know what led to this girl entering, but it seems reasonable to speculate from this reaction from her family that it might have been something that involved sexual shame.

Claire Keeley's Story – 1942

*A **Nurse** arrives at the Administration Office.*

Nurse   We had a death this morning on Ward 22.

Administrator   Name and number?

Nurse   Keeley. Claire Keeley. 19308.

*The **Administrator** retrieves the file.*

Administrator   Admitted 1908. Thirty-four years here.
Sixty-two years old. Cause of death?

Nurse   Cardiac failure.

Administrator   I'll inform the coroner. Next of kin?

Nurse   We had information on file in the ward. Husband
long dead. One son in London, last heard of about twelve
years ago. But there's a daughter in Dublin. We sent a
telegram. She'll attend the funeral. But she's unable to pay
for it.

*The **Administrator** finishes filling in the details in the Case Book,
and closes it.*

Final Meeting With a Historian

*The **Historian** returns. She now addresses the audience directly,
with no pretence of speaking to the students on stage.*

Historian   Why did we lock all these people up? There is no
simple answer. But let's go back to the famine. The people
who die during the famine – they're either landless or have
less than twenty acres of land. If you have twenty acres, your
prospects of survival are pretty good – you can sell a cow, you
have something to fall back on. So the lesson gets into people
that survival means holding on to the land. So one son gets
the land, one daughter marries locally, and the rest . . . They
either emigrate or, if they stay at home, they rattle around as
single people and are unable to marry, or they join the
church . . . It's a fairly ruthless family system. Mercenary.
People try to get relatives certified to just clear out the house
. . . to make space for someone else . . . to save money. It's
one less mouth to feed. You get your relatives
institutionalised and then you don't have to support them
any more. And so, if a woman in this society – or a girl – has a
child outside of marriage . . . well, she has to be cancelled, in
some way or other. Sometimes they might persuade

somebody to marry her. Sometimes her parents might take the child in – there was an awful lot of informal adoption. But these are the families that *have* some coping mechanisms. The ones that have nothing – they're the ones that end up in a workhouse, or a Magdalene Laundry, or in a mental hospital. And with the mental hospitals, if they went in, it was almost impossible to get them out. And if they tried to get out, it was impossible for them to find somewhere to go.

The End

The norms established for how the stage is lit and used now start to break down, gradually.

Mick *re-emerges.*

Mick   I went in to the psychiatric hospital voluntarily at the age of twenty-three or twenty-four, because it was my father's wish that I should. I felt a sense of rejection – like a woman who has an unplanned pregnancy, perhaps – I felt that from my father.

I arrived in to St Brendan's – the Gorman – on my birthday. It was roughly 1975, at a guess.

I remember standing in the corridor with my eyes closed, and another psychiatrist passed me by and blew gently into my face. I have a warm memory of him.

Brendan Kelly *re-emerges.*

Brendan Kelly   When I was a young psychiatrist I used occasionally have to visit patients in the old St Brendan's hospital. It was dark and it was damp and there were big empty buildings and old prefabs and there was very little space and very little light.

Mick   I was described as as a catatonic schizophrenic.

I remember saying to myself, well, if you want to take my freedom, you can take it all. When it came to getting up and getting dressed in the morning, I wouldn't do anything. It was a kind of peaceful resistance – like Mahatma Gandhi. I never lifted my hand to anybody. I just didn't believe in pointless exercise. You wake up in the morning, somebody wants you to get out of the bed so they can make the bed – well, I wouldn't get out of my bed till I was free to make my own. If they wanted me to get up, they would have to dress me. If they wanted me to go to a table, they would have to lead me to the table. I was observing these things.

Brendan Kelly   When you go out of here, today, and you observe the beautiful landscaping, the light, the lovely buildings – the sense of *openness* – that's probably what it felt like when it opened in 1814. It was a beautiful institution. It was built in a spirit of very great therapeutic optimism – this absolute belief in the power of institutions to cure and to help and to fix society.

Mick   I was transferred to 8B – a locked ward. It was notorious. People walked around all day inside the ward tapping cigarettes off each other, picking butts up off the floor – think of a lion in a lion cage, in the zoo.

We used to say the rosary. One fellow was a bank robber. There was another fellow there who's shot somebody in the English army. They were very happy to join in.

Electro-convulsive therapy – ECT – it was used as a means of correction – I knew a gentleman who was given ECT because he set the crib on fire.

I spent thirty-four days in Ward 8B. Then I was transferred back to the main ward.

Brendan Kelly   I look at this new light-filled, space-filled campus with . . . such sadness, because I know patients lived their lives in a very cramped, confined, darkened version of this, and those lives could have been lived in a place the way it looks today.

But that institution is gone, and that is a good, cold, hard fact. That systemic change has been huge – and the spaciousness you feel outside in the campus, now, is a reflection of that.

So there is hope. But it is tinged with sadness for opportunities lost in the past. It could have been like this all along.

Mick   I left the Gorman on the feast of St Francis of Assisi. You could go out for the day – if you had a day pass – and there was a bed check at 8.30 at night when they'd check if everybody was there. I was out for the day and I was late going back and I realised I had missed the bed check. So there was no need to go back. So I went to a Christian student house I knew of and they gave me accommodation. And . . . I never went back.

A series of patients emerge.

Patient One

Dear Sir,
I wish to give in seventy-two hours' notice from today.
I am feeling perfectly well again and am most anxious to get home.

Patient Two

Dear Doctor,
I wish to tender seventy-two hours' notice, as I feel well enough to resume work.

Patient Three

Dear Sir,
Being a voluntary patient I wish to send in seventy-two hours' notice for discharge from this date. I think that I am on the road to recovery with God's power.

Patient Four

Dear Charlie,
I wanted to let you know I arrived in London safely, delighted to say am feeling tip-top. I must say it's great to be free again, this time I shall be very wise, no more nonsense. So far no job, but tomorrow I shall go all round

see what's cooking. I hope you are keeping up your heart and on your own way out of the Gorman.

Patient Five
Dear Doctor,
A short line to let you know that I am keeping go h-iontáil sláintiúl since I left. I can never forget the great work you are supervising in Grange Gorman. Thanks a thousand times to you, and your wonderful electric shock treatment.

Mick   One of the reasons I believe there was so much admission to the mental hospitals is that people were being asked to live up to a false person – not themselves. They were being asked to conform to something that wasn't themselves. They were in here because they had problems being themselves.

My life has been – most of it – puzzled by the reaction of people. I've always found it difficult to understand where people are at . . .

I would always be asking, why am I doing this? What's the best thing to do here? Everything I did, I did according to intuition or feeling. I was working out my own pathway to peace. I was on a journey.

Beat.

What I was really trying to get to the nub of was: why am I doing anything other than out of fear? I eventually decided: I am *not* going to act out of fear.

Epilogue

Teacher   And – scene. Well done everybody.

They relax.

Student   How are we going to end this?

Teacher   The way we do every class. With a bit of self-care. Ok everyone, let's take it back in.

They gather in a circle.

The **Teacher** *calls on one of the students to lead the warm-down – a simple, short ritual with which they finish each class. The* **Student** *does so, culminating in general applause and upbeat chat as the class breaks up and disperses.*

Teacher (*reminding them*)   Don't forget to tidy up.

A few remain behind to re-box and remove the research materials.

Amidst this, the **Student Actress** *from earlier calls back the* **Student Actor**.

Student Actress   Hey – have you got a few minutes – would you look at my monologue for my showcase?

Student Actor   Sure. What are you doing?

The general lighting starts to fade, almost imperceptibly. The tidying-up may continue in the fading light as the **Student Actress** *delivers her monologue. Eventually, the light should fade to a spot, with only the* **Student Actress** *visible.*

Student Actress   I think you'll recognise it.

She plays this inflected with all that she has learned of the women who passed through Grangegorman – playing it not as Hamlet, but as a character who has wrestled with her own mental health, who has faced the ultimate question, who has scars to heal and losses to mourn, but who is fighting on.

Student Actress
To be, or not to be, that is the question:
Whether 'tis nobler in the mind to suffer
The slings and arrows of outrageous fortune,
Or to take arms against a sea of troubles
And by opposing end them. To die – to sleep,
No more; and by a sleep to say we end
The heart-ache and the thousand natural shocks
That flesh is heir to: 'tis a consummation
Devoutly to be wished. To die, to sleep;
To sleep, perchance to dream – ay, there's the rub;

For in that sleep of death what dreams may come,
When we have shuffled off this mortal coil,
Must give us pause – there's the respect
That makes calamity of so long life.
For who would bear the whips and scorns of time,
The oppressor's wrong, the proud man's contumely,
The pangs of despised love, the law's delay,
The insolence of office, and the spurns
That patient merit of the unworthy takes,
When he himself might his quietus make
With a bare bodkin? Who would fardels bear,
To grunt and sweat under a weary life,
But that the dread of something after death,
The undiscovered country, from whose bourn
No traveller returns, puzzles the will,
And makes us rather bear those ills we have
Than fly to others that we know not of?
Thus conscience does make cowards of us all,
And thus the native hue of resolution
Is sicklied o'er with the pale cast of thought,
And enterprises of great pith and moment
With this regard their currents turn awry
And lose the name of action –

Ophelia *has appeared, caught in a beam or flicker of light.*

Student Actress
    Soft you now,
    The fair Ophelia!

*Their eyes lock. In that moment is the possibility of an entirely
different story for* **Ophelia** *– one where she is embraced and
empowered – the story she would write herself.*

Blackout.

Ends.

Afterword

At some point in the early 2000s, I became aware of
Grangegorman. We moved to Cabra, and I 'found'
Grangegorman Lower Road, which seemed incongruously
rural, and managed to be both idyllic and eerie. Journalistic
work brought me into contact with its history and with
people who had passed through it; one of those stories
became an essay for the *Dublin Review*; another, I haven't yet
been able to write. In 2011, a documentary by Mary Raftery,
Behind the Walls, revealed the existence of an apparently
forgotten archive of documents and artefacts, and inspired
community efforts to save it. Then, in 2014, I visited the
artist Alan Counihan's exhibition of a selection of those
artefacts, *Personal Effects: A History of Possession*, and
interviewed him for an article. The following year, the
playground and the jogging path on the campus opened,
and Grangegorman began to take on another, more
intimate, meaning for me. I have spent many hours pushing
swings, running around the track and enjoying the
surprising views across to the hills. All this is to say that when
Peter McDermott and Tanya Dean of the TU Dublin
Conservatoire approached me to ask me to write a play
based on and set in Grangegorman, for their students, it
didn't take me long to say yes.

I have written a series of plays about Irish history and
politics, all – to greater or lesser degree – documentary in
nature. Most of them have been set in the corridors of power
or been about access to those corridors. Mostly, they have
been – in the first instance – about men. Mostly, they have
been about decisions made, on which history turned. When
I need help marshalling that history, I turn to Aristotle, and
Joseph Campbell, and Robert McKee. I look for unities, and
the hero's journey, and an inciting incident and crisis point.
When I started working on this play, I did that again. I read
the histories first: they were full of men going on journeys
and making decisions. Ivor Browne's accounts of his time
working at, and later running, St Brendan's are incredibly

compelling; I thought the play might be about him, or about successive directors of the hospital. Still, the scope of the story seemed vast.

Then I went into the archive. It took me a day to work out even where to find anything: most records I initially requested were bureaucratic and unenlightening. And then I found the Female Case Book for 1908: an immense, leather-bound volume with a new page for every new admission, page upon page of carefully handwritten case notes, and perfectly preserved studio portraits of each of the women admitted that year. I realised that this play could not be about the people who ran the institution – the people who wrote the history, or whom the history was written about. The point of it had to be to bring the unwritten stories (or, perhaps, the unread stories) to life. But if the official history of the institution was vast, the entire history of those who passed through it was vaster again. How to find dramatic coherence in that history? How to impose narrative order on that archive? The Case Book contained page after page of pathos; there was plenty of tragedy, in the generic sense in which we use the word today, to mean merely 'sadness'. But it wasn't clear that there was anything like tragedy in the sense that Aristotle, or Shakespeare, or Arthur Miller, or Sean O'Casey understood it, where the tragic fate of the protagonist is somehow consequent upon their character or their actions. Some of the women in that Case Book got better, were discharged and disappeared from the record; others died in Grangegorman, with only the barest of accounts of their decline and death. What the Case Book couldn't tell us was how they felt about their lives; whether they had dreams or regrets; whether they had agency; whether they were defeated, or struggled on, or were simply ill. It all seemed very random.

I started to transcribe records and brought selections to the students to watch them workshop them with Peter and Tanya. We talked about them. Peter and I videoed those conversations and transcribed some of them. I started to think that the way we were all struggling with this material, and the way this new generation of 'residents' of Grangegorman were responding to it, was illuminating of itself, and somehow dramatic. I thought perhaps the students could play themselves on stage. I remembered Alan Counihan's exhibition and how he had described his own discovery and sifting of the archive. I borrowed that conceit and gave it to the students. I had seen the previous year's students perform *The Laramie Project* by Moisés Kaufman and the Tectonic Theater Project, which itself is not unlike some of David Hare's documentary theatre, and thought that that fragmentary quality could work. I thought of other attempts to portray 'madness' on stage and screen, and how poorly they have aged. I began to knit all this together – all the while testing these ideas with Peter and Tanya, and refining them based on their suggestions.

I was never quite sure we had a 'play'. Perhaps that's the nature of this particular documentary material – its vastness, its foreignness in time, its silences and its fragmentary quality conspire to defeat the attempt to impose 'narrative' on it. And so, as I wrestled with this, that – in part – is what the play became: the story of the attempt to impose narrative on something that defies narrative. A workshop.